# Tech Giants and
# Digital Domination

# Other Books of Related Interest

**GLOBAL**VIEWPOINTS

# Tech Giants and Digital Domination

*Caleb Bissinger, Book Editor*

GREENHAVEN
PUBLISHING

Published in 2018 by Greenhaven Publishing, LLC
353 3rd Avenue, Suite 255, New York, NY 10010

Articles in Greenhaven Publishing anthologies are often edited for length to meet page
requirements. In addition, original titles of these works are changed to clearly present
the main thesis and to explicitly indicate the author's opinion. Every effort is made to
ensure that Greenhaven Publishing accurately reflects the original intent of the authors.
Every effort has been made to trace the owners of the copyrighted material.

Cover image: Zhang Peng/LightRocket via Getty Images
Map: frees/Shutterstock.com

### Cataloging-in-Publication Data

Names: Bissinger, Caleb, editor.
Title: Tech giants and digital domination / edited by Caleb Bissinger.
Description: New York : Greenhaven Publishing, 2018. | Series: Global viewpoints | Includes
  bibliographical references and index. | Audience: Grades 9-12.
Identifiers: LCCN ISBN 9781534501256 (library bound) | ISBN 9781534501232 (pbk.)
Subjects: LCSH: Technological innovations--Economic aspects. | Industries—Technological
  innovations.
Classification: LCC HC79.T4 T43 2018 | DDC 338.064—dc23

*Manufactured in the United States of America*

Website: http://greenhavenpublishing.com

# Contents

## Chapter 1: Tech Giants Worldwide

# Chapter 2: Technology's Mark on Our World

# Chapter 3: Tech Giants and Corporate Social Responsibility

## Chapter 4: Are We Headed for a Technocracy?

# Foreword

Global interdependence has become an undeniable reality. Mass media and technology have increased worldwide access to information and created a society of global citizens. Understanding and navigating this global community is a challenge, requiring a high degree of information literacy and a new level of learning sophistication.

Building on the success of its flagship series, Opposing Viewpoints, Greenhaven Publishing has created the Global Viewpoints series to examine a broad range of current, often controversial topics of worldwide importance from a variety of international perspectives. Providing students and other readers with the information they need to explore global connections and think critically about worldwide implications, each Global Viewpoints volume offers a panoramic view of a topic of widespread significance.

Drugs, famine, immigration—a broad, international treatment is essential to do justice to social, environmental, health, and political issues such as these. Junior high, high school, and early college students, as well as general readers, can all use Global Viewpoints anthologies to discern the complexities relating to each issue. Readers will be able to examine unique national perspectives while, at the same time, appreciating the interconnectedness that global priorities bring to all nations and cultures.

Material in each volume is selected from a diverse range of sources, including journals, magazines, newspapers, nonfiction books, speeches, government documents, pamphlets, organization newsletters, and position papers. Global Viewpoints is truly global, with material drawn primarily from international sources available in English and secondarily from US sources with extensive international coverage.

Features of each volume in the Global Viewpoints series include:

- An **annotated table of contents** that provides a brief summary of each essay in the volume, including the name of the country or area covered in the essay.

- An **introduction** specific to the volume topic.

- For each viewpoint, an **introduction** that contains notes about the author and source of the viewpoint explains why material from the specific country is being presented, summarizes the main points of the viewpoint, and offers three **guided reading questions** to aid in understanding and comprehension.

- **For further discussion** questions that promote critical thinking by asking the reader to compare and contrast aspects of the viewpoints or draw conclusions about perspectives and arguments.

- A worldwide list of **organizations to contact** for readers seeking additional information.

- A **periodical bibliography** for each chapter and a **bibliography of books** on the volume topic to aid in further research.

- A comprehensive **subject index** to offer access to people, places, events, and subjects cited in the text.

Global Viewpoints is designed for a broad spectrum of readers who want to learn more about current events, history, political science, government, international relations, economics, environmental science, world cultures, and sociology—students doing research for class assignments or debates, teachers and faculty seeking to supplement course materials, and others wanting to understand current issues better. By presenting how people in various countries perceive the root causes, current consequences, and proposed solutions to worldwide challenges, Global Viewpoints volumes offer readers opportunities to enhance their global awareness and their knowledge of cultures worldwide.

# Introduction

> *"There is little doubt that the genie is out of the bottle and the world must adapt and adopt technologies even if they destroy the old to create new products, jobs and business models."*
> Diane Francis, National Post

One day in 1901, a group of Greek divers went looking for sea sponges near the isle of Antikythera and found a 2,000-year-old shipwreck instead. Among the ruins were three bronze lumps. Anything that survives two millennia soaking in the Aegean is remarkable for its hardiness. These shards garnered heightened admiration. They housed toothed gears, which weren't supposed to have been invented until a thousand years *after* the ship sank, and they had grooved rings, like a track for some missing appendage, suggesting they were once part of an elaborate apparatus. Archaeologists determined that the device, in its totality, measured planetary movements. The technological precociousness of this was befuddling. Some said there could only be one explanation: aliens. Today, another theory prevails. The Antikythera mechanism is considered the world's oldest computer.

So how did we get here from there? How did a celestial tracker evolve into the iPhone, bits of bronze into autonomous vehicles? Try to isolate an element of your life that isn't somehow informed by technology. Can you? Go back in time, a few years, a decade. Are there devices now—in your home, in your pocket, indispensable perhaps—that didn't exist then?

New technology comes at us with the indiscriminate hunger of a forest fire. Wearable devices herald a new premise of proximate connectivity. Self-driving cars are the first stitch in the autonomous blanket. A recent study by the University of Oxford concludes that 47 percent of jobs in the United States could be automated away in the next two decades. As one observer, Kevin Maney, has put it: "[Artificial intelligence] will lead us into the mother of all tech revolutions. The last time anything came close was around 1900, when the automobile, telecommunications, the airplane and mass electrification all came together at once, radically changing the world from the late 1800s to the 1920s. Such times are particularly frightening."

The viewpoints in this book will help you make sense of technology's stampede and what it means for you as a citizen, student, and consumer.

When we talk about technology, we're not just talking about computers and smartphones. The word encompasses anything that is engineered to alleviate labor, expedite access, or improve existing tools. Change—what those in Silicon Valley like to call *disruption*—is the underlying principle, and tech pioneers have excitable metabolisms; their desire to improve, enhance, and reinvent is primal. Innovation—to make new—is their watchword, but, as this book will often ask you to consider, at what cost? Technology can be frivolous ("Do we really need an app for that?"), but it can also be profound. Social media targets the very essence of humanity—communication. Self-driving cars, which are expected to number 10 million by the end of the decade, won't just change how we get from A to B, they'll eradicate one of the last century's most romantic images: a driver, a car, and the open road. Technology can be subtle, too: trashcans that tell the waste department when they're full or power grids that counsel home appliances on energy conservation.

This may all seem rather utopian, but it is bounded by perils. ("Utopia," after all, means "no place.") Rather than an expansive terrain of competing views, social medial is, for many, a cul-de-sac of preconceived notions. Sure, autonomous cars may lighten traffic, but what happens when one faces a lose-lose scenario, like driving into a wall to avoid a pedestrian? Whose ethics should the car adhere to—government regulators, auto manufacturers, or the vehicle's owners? Who teaches an autonomous anything how to think?

Consider this: One thing we know for certain about our technological future is that there will be an absurd amount of data. Internet-enabled devices in 10,000 homes generate 150 million data points every day. Such abundance makes it all but impossible to distinguish between innocuous and sensitive datum. How do you safeguard privacy as tech companies steward more and more personal information?

The omnipresence of tech companies has given their founders a platform for idealistic ambition. But under that paradigm, as the line between corporate interest and social responsibility blurs, how do you separate what counts as genuine advocacy from what is merely meant to benefit the company's bottom line?

An old show tune goes: "They all laughed at Christopher Columbus when he said the world was round. / They all laughed when Edison recorded sound. / They all laughed at Wilbur and his brother when they said that man could fly. ... / Who's got the last laugh now?" It's easy to scoff at newfangled things, easier still to be oblivious. The purpose of this book is to draw you into the vital conversations that are happening every day about what technology means for global well-being.

The viewpoints that follow take on a wide range of topics, from the relationship between technology and terrorism to the political dimensions of social media's preeminence; from the interplay between ethics and engineering to the thunderous might of artificial intelligence. Technology is rapidly reshaping our world, and *Tech Giants and Digital Domination* will help you reconcile the wonders with the implications.

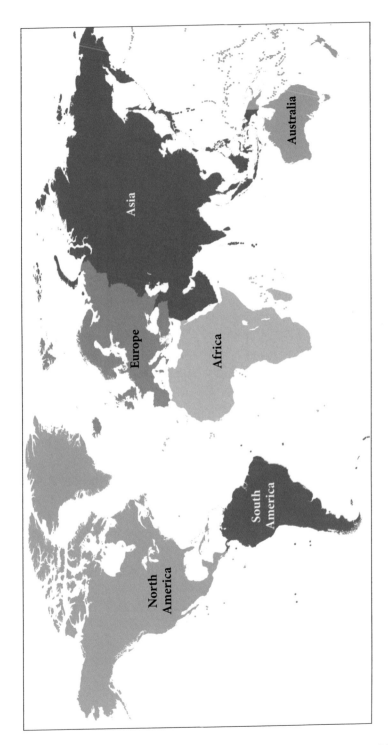

# CHAPTER 1

# Tech Giants Worldwide

# The Increasing Power of Tech Giants

*Bradley Love*

*In the following viewpoint, Bradley Love argues that we should be wary of playing in to tech industry hype. A warning issued by several industry leaders regarding the potential threat of artificial intelligence (AI) was cause for alarm for many. However, Love argues, we should consider the motives and interests of these tech giants, who have cast themselves in the very important position of determining our future. While Love concedes that AI could indeed present certain real dangers, he argues that we would be wise to keep a level head and look to our elected representatives and other leaders for perspective. Love is professor of cognitive and decision sciences at University College London and an inaugural faculty fellow at the Alan Turing Institute, the UK's national institute for data science.*

As you read, consider the following questions:

1. Which renowned physicist issued a public warning about AI?
2. For what reason does the author believe AI is more likely to go wrong?
3. What example does the author suggest is a potential real danger that could be brought about by AI?

S tar physicist Stephen Hawking has reiterated his concerns that the rise of powerful artificial intelligence (AI) systems could spell the end for humanity. Speaking at the launch of the University of Cambridge's Centre for the Future of Intelligence on 19 October, he did, however, acknowledge that AI equally has the potential to be one of the best things that could happen to us.

So are we on the cusp of creating super-intelligent machines that could put humanity at existential risk?

There are those who believe that AI will be a boom for humanity, improving health services and productivity as well as freeing us from mundane tasks. However, the most vocal leaders in academia and industry are convinced that the danger of our own creations turning on us is real. For example, Elon Musk, founder of Tesla Motors and SpaceX, has set up a billion-dollar non-profit company with contributions from tech titans, such as Amazon, to prevent an evil AI from bringing about the end of humanity. Universities, such as Berkeley, Oxford and Cambridge have established institutes to address the issue. Luminaries like Bill Joy, Bill Gates and Ray Kurzweil have all raised the alarm.

Listening to this, it seems the end may indeed be nigh unless we act before it's too late.

## The Role of the Tech Industry

Or could it be that science fiction and industry-fuelled hype have simply overcome better judgement? The cynic might say that the AI doomsday vision has taken on religious proportions. Of course, doomsday visions usually come with a path to salvation. Accordingly, Kurzweil claims we will be virtually immortal soon through nanobots that will digitise our memories. And Musk recently proclaimed that it's a near certainty that we are simulations within a computer akin to The Matrix, offering the possibility of a richer encompassing reality where our "programs" can be preserved and reconfigured for centuries.

Tech giants have cast themselves as modern gods with the power to either extinguish humanity or make us immortal through

## Why Virtual Reality, Wearable Tech, and Intelligent Personal Assistants Are Failing to Catch On

**Kai Ryssdal:** Is it possible that VR is just ahead of its time, that we haven't figured out the interface thing yet?

**Molly Wood:** It's sort of ironic, because VR has actually been around for 75 years or more. … It's kind of just always been ahead of its time, and it's still a hard sell. … It's isolating, you have to sort of sit by yourself or rearrange your entire man-cave around the virtual reality set up. There's limited content, the tech isn't perfect and it makes people nauseous. I mean, there are a lot of really significant barriers to adoption. And then on top of that, when we have so many sources of entertainment in our lives, I think people are still trying to come up with a reason why they need it.

**Ryssdal:** Yeah, and there's other stuff in that category too, right?

**Wood:** There's a ton of technology in that category and always has been. And I think you could look around the tech market and say wearables are actually—despite all of the hype—in a really similar position as a virtual reality. …You know, it's a cycle but it's not a cycle that says "I desperately have to have this." … But it's not just that. The internet of things has been way slower to take off than people thought. And, mark my words, that is a category that's going to take much longer than people expected. …

The Amazon Echo is basically for kids, and for setting timers for kids, and the research bears that out. People stop using it after a couple of months. So if necessity is the mother of invention, I think the tech industry thinks that invention is the mother of invention—"we will make it and you will buy it."

*"Oculus pop-up closings signal trouble in virtual reality market," Kai Ryssdal and Molly Wood, Marketplace, February 9, 2017.*

their brilliance. This binary vision is buoyed in the tech world because it feeds egos—what conceit could be greater than believing one's work could usher in such rapid innovation that history as we know it ends? No longer are tech figures cast as mere business leaders, but instead as the chosen few who will determine the future of humanity and beyond.

For Judgement Day researchers, proclamations of an "existential threat" is not just a call to action, but also attracts generous funding and an opportunity to rub shoulders with the tech elite.

So, are smart machines more likely to kill us, save us, or simply drive us to work? To answer this question, it helps to step back and look at what is actually happening in AI.

## Underneath the Hype

The basic technologies, such as those recently employed by Google's DeepMind to defeat a human expert at the game Go, are simply refinements of technologies developed in the 1980s. There have been no qualitative breakthroughs in approach. Instead, performance gains are attributable to larger training sets (also known as big data) and increased processing power. What is unchanged is that most machine systems work by maximising some kind of objective. In a game, the objective is simply to win, which is formally defined (for example capture the king in chess). This is one reason why games (checkers, chess, Go) are AI mainstays—it's easy to specify the objective function.

In other cases, it may be harder to define the objective and this is where AI could go wrong. However, AI is more likely to go wrong for reasons of incompetence rather than malice. For example, imagine that the US nuclear arsenal during the Cold War was under control of an AI to thwart sneak attack by the Soviet Union. Due to no action of the Soviet Union, a nuclear reactor meltdown occurs in the arsenal and the power grid temporarily collapses. The AI's sensors detect the disruption and fallout, leading the system to infer an attack is underway. The president instructs the system in a shaky voice to stand down, but the AI takes the troubled voice as evidence the president is being coerced. Missiles released. End of humanity.

The AI was simply following its programming, which led to a catastrophic error. This is exactly the kind of deadly mistakes that humans almost made during the Cold War. Our destruction would be attributable to our own incompetence rather than an evil AI turning on us—no different than an auto-pilot malfunctioning on a jumbo jet and sending its unfortunate passengers to their doom. In contrast, human pilots have purposefully killed their passengers, so perhaps we should welcome self-driving cars.

Of course, humans could design AIs to kill, but again this is people killing each other, not some self-aware machine. Western governments have already released computer viruses, such as Stuxnet, to target critical industrial infrastructure. Future viruses could be more clever and deadly. However, this essentially follows the arc of history where humans use available technologies to kill one another.

There are real dangers from AI but they tend to be economic and social in nature. Clever AI will create tremendous wealth for society, but will leave many people without jobs. Unlike the industrial revolution, there may not be jobs for segments of society as machines may be better at every possible job. There will not be a flood of replacement "AI repair person" jobs to take up the slack. So the real challenge will be how to properly assist those (most of us?) who are displaced by AI. Another issue will be the fact that people will not look after one another as machines permanently displace entire classes of labour, such as healthcare workers.

Fortunately, the governments may prove more level-headed than tech celebrities if they choose to listen to nuanced advice. A recent report by the UK's House of Commons Science and Technology Committee on the risks of AI, for example, focuses on economic, social and ethical concerns. The take-home message was that AI will make industry more efficient, but may also destabilise society.

If we are going to worry about the future of humanity we should focus on the real challenges, such as climate change and weapons of mass destruction rather than fanciful killer AI robots.

# Social Media Has Swallowed Journalism

*Emily Bell*

*In the following viewpoint, Emily Bell addresses social media as a roaring news platform. Discover on Snapchat, Moments on Twitter, Instant Articles on Facebook—these venues give traditional outlets incredible access to news seekers. But by allowing tech companies to distribute and promote content as they (or their algorithms) see fit, news agencies may undermine their ability to stay profitable, relevant, and cohesive. Bell wonders if social media platforms are more powerful than their content and proposes some ways news organizations can adapt to the new media ecosystem. Bell is director of the Tow Center for Digital Journalism at Columbia Journalism School.*

As you read, consider the following questions:

1. What percentage of adults in America consider Facebook to be a news source?
2. What is native advertising?
3. Does the author believe there is a stable future for for-profit news outlets?

Something really dramatic is happening to our media landscape, the public sphere, and our journalism industry, almost without us noticing and certainly without the level of public examination

"Facebook Is Eating the World," by Emily Bell, Columbia Journalism Review, March 7, 2016. Reprinted by permission.

and debate it deserves. Our news ecosystem has changed more dramatically in the past five years than perhaps at any time in the past five hundred. We are seeing huge leaps in technical capability—virtual reality, live video, artificially intelligent news bots, instant messaging, and chat apps. We are seeing massive changes in control, and finance, putting the future of our publishing ecosystem into the hands of a few, who now control the destiny of many.

Social media hasn't just swallowed journalism, it has swallowed everything. It has swallowed political campaigns, banking systems, personal histories, the leisure industry, retail, even government and security. The phone in our pocket is our portal to the world. I think in many ways this heralds enormously exciting opportunities for education, information, and connection, but it brings with it a host of contingent existential risks.

Journalism is a small subsidiary activity of the main business of social platforms, but one of central interest to citizens.

The internet and the social Web enable journalists to do powerful work, while at the same time helping to make the business of publishing journalism an uneconomic venture.

Two significant things have already happened that we have not paid enough attention to:

First, news publishers have lost control over distribution.

Social media and platform companies took over what publishers couldn't have built even if they wanted to. Now the news is filtered through algorithms and platforms which are opaque and unpredictable. The news business is embracing this trend, and digital native entrants like BuzzFeed, Vox, and Fusion have built their presence on the premise that they are working within this system, not against it.

Second, the inevitable outcome of this is the increase in power of social media companies.

The largest of the platform and social media companies, Google, Apple, Facebook, Amazon, and even second order companies such as Twitter, Snapchat and emerging messaging app companies, have become extremely powerful in terms of controlling who publishes what to whom, and how that publication is monetized.

There is a far greater concentration of power in this respect than there ever has been in the past. Networks favor economies of scale, so our careful curation of plurality in media markets such as the UK, disappears at a stroke, and the market dynamics and anti-trust laws the Americans rely on to sort out such anomalies are failing.

The mobile revolution is behind much of this.

Because of the revolution in mobile, the amount of time we spend online, the number of things we do online, and the attention we spend on platforms has exploded.

The design and capabilities of our phones (thank you, Apple) favor apps, which foster different behavior. Google did recent research through its Android platform that showed, while we might have an average of 25 apps on our phones, we only use four or five of those apps every day, and of those apps we use every day, the most significant chunk of our time is spent on a social media app. And at the moment the reach of Facebook is far greater than any other social platform.

The majority of American adults are Facebook users, and the majority of those users regularly get some kind of news from Facebook, which according to Pew Research Center data, means that around 40 percent of US adults overall consider Facebook a source of news.

So let's recap:

1.  People are increasingly using their smartphones for everything.

2.  They do it mostly through apps, and in particular social and messaging apps, such as Facebook, WhatsApp, Snapchat, and Twitter.

3.  The competition to become such an app is intense. Competitive advantage for platforms relies on being able to keep your users within an app. The more your users are within your app, the more you know about them, the

more that information can then be used to sell advertising, the higher your revenues. The competition for attention is fierce. The "four horsemen of the apocalypse"— Google, Facebook, Apple, and Amazon (five if you add in Microsoft)—are engaged in a prolonged and torrid war over whose technologies, platforms, and even ideologies will win.

In the last year, journalists and news publishers have therefore unexpectedly found themselves the beneficiaries of this conflict.

In the past year, Snapchat launched its Discover App, giving channels to brands like Vice, BuzzFeed, the *Wall Street Journal*, *Cosmo*, and the Daily Mail. Facebook launched Instant Articles, which it recently announced will be opened up to all publishers in April. Apple and Google quickly followed suit, launching Apple News and Accelerated Mobile Pages, respectively. Not wanting to be left out, Twitter also launched its own Moments, an aggregation of trending material on the platform to tell complete stories about events.

It is very good news that well-resourced platform companies are designing systems that distribute news. But as one door opens, another one is closing.

At the same time that publishers are being enticed to publish directly into apps and new systems, which will rapidly grow their mobile audiences, Apple announced it would allow ad-blocking software to be downloaded from its App store.

In other words, if as a publisher your alternative to going onto a distributed platform is to make money through mobile advertising, anyone on an iPhone can now block all ads and their invidious tracking software. Articles that appear within platforms, such as Discover on Snapchat or Instant Articles on Facebook, are largely, though not totally, immune from blockers. Effectively, the already very small share of mobile digital advertising publishers might be getting independently from mobile is potentially cut out. Of course, one might add that publishers had it coming from weighing down their pages with intrusive ads nobody wanted in the first place.

There are three alternatives for commercial publishers.

One is to push even more of your journalism straight to an app like Facebook and its Instant Articles where ad blocking is not impossible but harder than at the browser level. As one publisher put it to me, "We look at the amount we might make from mobile and we suspect that even if we gave everything straight to Facebook, we would still be better off." The risks, though, in being reliant on the revenue and traffic from one distributor, are very high.

The second option is to build other businesses and revenues away from distributed platforms. Accept that seeking a vast audience through other platforms is not only *not* helping you but actively damaging your journalism, so move to a measurement of audience engagement rather than scale.

Membership or subscription are most commonly considered in this context. Ironically, the prerequisites for this are having a strong brand identity that subscribers feel affinity towards. In a world where content is highly distributed, this is far harder to achieve than when it is tied to packaged physical products. Even in the handful of cases where subscription is working, it is often not making up the shortfall in advertising.

The third is, of course, to make advertising that doesn't look like advertising at all, so ad blockers can't detect it. This used to be called "advertorial" or "sponsorship," but now is known as "native advertising," and it has grown to nearly a quarter of all digital display advertising in the US. In fact, digitally native companies like BuzzFeed, Vox, and hybrids like Vice, have disrupted the failing publishing model by essentially becoming advertising agencies—which are themselves in danger of failing. What I mean by this is that they deal directly with advertisers, they make the kind of viral video films and GIFs we see scattered all over our Facebook pages, and then they publish them to all those people who have previously "liked" or shared other material from that publisher.

The logical answer reached by many publishers to much of this is to invest in their own destination apps. But as we have seen, even your own app has to be compliant with the distribution standards of others in order to work. And investing in maintaining your own presence comes at a time when advertising (particularly in print) is under pressure, and online advertising is not growing either. The critical balance between destination and distribution is probably the hardest investment decision traditional publishers have to make right now.

Publishers are reporting that Instant Articles are giving them maybe three or four times the traffic they would expect. The temptation for publishers to go "all in" on distributed platforms, and just start creating journalism and stories that work on the social Web, is getting stronger. I can imagine we will see news companies totally abandoning production capacity, technology capacity, and even advertising departments, and delegating it all to third-party platforms in an attempt to stay afloat.

This is a high-risk strategy: You lose control over your relationship with your readers and viewers, your revenue, and even the path your stories take to reach their destination.

With billions of users and hundreds of thousands of articles, pictures, and videos arriving online everyday, social platforms have to employ algorithms to try and sort through the *important* and *recent* and *popular* and decide who ought to see what. And we have no option but to trust them to do this.

In truth, we have little or no insight into how each company is sorting its news. If Facebook decides, for instance, that video stories will do better than text stories, we cannot know that unless they tell us or unless we observe it. This is an unregulated field. There is no transparency into the internal working of these systems.

There are huge benefits to having a new class of technically able, socially aware, financially successful, and highly energetic people like Mark Zuckerberg taking over functions and economic power from some of the staid, politically entrenched, and occasionally corrupt gatekeepers we have had in the past. But we ought to be aware, too, that this cultural, economic, and political shift is profound.

We are handing the controls of important parts of our public and private lives to a very small number of people, who are unelected and unaccountable.

We need regulation to make sure all citizens gain equal access to the networks of opportunity and services they need. We also need to know that all public speech and expression will be treated transparently, even if they cannot be treated equally. This is a basic requirement for a functioning democracy.

For this to happen, there has to be at least some agreement that the responsibilities in this area are shifting. The people who built these platform companies did not set out to do so in order to take over the responsibilities of a free press. In fact, they are rather alarmed that this is the outcome of their engineering success.

One of the criticisms thus far leveled against these companies is that they have cherry-picked the profitable parts of the publishing process and sidestepped the more expensive business of actually creating good journalism. If the current nascent experiments such as Instant Articles lead to a more integrated relationship with journalism, it is possible that we will see a more significant shift of production costs follow, particularly around technology and advertising sales.

The reintermediation of information, which once looked as though it was going to be fully democratized by the progress of the open Web, is likely to make the mechanisms for funding journalism worse before they get better. Looking at the prospects for mobile advertising and the aggressive growth targets Apple, Facebook, Google, and the rest have to meet to satisfy Wall Street, it is fair to say that unless social platforms return a great deal more money back to the source, producing news is likely to become a nonprofit pursuit rather than an engine of capitalism.

To be sustainable, news and journalism companies will need to radically alter their cost base. It seems most likely that the next wave of news media companies will be fashioned around a studio model of managing different stories, talents, and products across a vast range of devices and platforms. As this shift happens, posting journalism directly to Facebook or other platforms will become the rule rather than the exception. Even maintaining a website could be abandoned in favor of hyperdistribution. The distinction between platforms and publishers will melt completely.

Even if you think of yourself as a technology company, you are making critical decisions about everything from access to platforms, the shape of journalism or speech, the inclusion or banning of certain content, the acceptance or rejection of various publishers.

What happens to the current class of news publishers is a much less important question than what kind of a news and information society we want to create and how can we help shape this.

# Amazon Has Been the Model of Disruption

*Susan Reda*

*In the following viewpoint Susan Reda charts the steps Amazon took to become the ultimate disruptor. The principle of disruption was first pegged by Clayton Christensen, a professor at Harvard Business School, in his 1992 book,* The Innovator's Dilemma. *The idea is that innovation obviates existing technology. Disruptors don't just ask new questions: they change the conversation. (The theory has its detractors. Christensen famously predicted the iPhone would fail because it wasn't disruptive enough; his critics point out that the genius of the device is that it marries old forms—a phone that's also a calendar that's also a music player that's also a video screen—rather than obliterating them.) Reda looks at the novel ideas—among them one-click shopping, voice-activated ordering, and drone delivery— that helped Amazon succeed in e-commerce. Reda is the editor of* Stores Media.

As you read, consider the following questions:

1. What patent did Amazon secure in 1997?
2. How does Amazon's customer outreach create an aura of transparency?
3. What percentage of American households can Amazon deliver to in an hour or less?

Turning 21 is considered a rite of passage in most Americans' lives; it signifies a transition into adulthood and a passage from years of schooling to a journey of countless responsibilities.

Amazon.com turned 21 this summer, and it's fair to say the Seattle-based e-commerce giant is handling the transition with aplomb. In July its market capitalization hit $356 billion, positioning it as the fifth-most-valuable U.S.-listed company; that same month, the second iteration of Amazon Prime Day yielded a 60 percent bump in sales over 2015.

While CEO Jeff Bezos' model was originally focused on growth over profitability, that has changed, too. The company recently reported its third quarter of record profits, achieving $857 million in income.

"Amazon is a case study in ceaseless innovation and interminable disruption," says Artemis Berry, vice president of digital retail for Shop.org and the National Retail Federation. "There have been numerous firsts just since the start of this year, including new private label brands, redefined logistics and the debut of online shopping by voice. They have truly earned the nickname of 'ultimate disrupter.'"

To toast Amazon's 21st birthday, STORES uncovered 21 times it changed the dynamics of selling, came up with fundamental new ways of doing business and altered how customer satisfaction is measured.

## Once Upon a Time

One of the earliest signs that Amazon would be a disrupter to be reckoned with was 1-Click Shopping. Introduced in 1997, 1-Click eliminated the need for shoppers to re-enter payment information every time they made a purchase.

"It eliminated that redundancy of having to key in field after field of personal payment information," says Jason Goldberg, senior vice president of content and commerce at Razorfish. "We take for granted today how quick it is to log in, choose an item and buy it with just one click, but it was so unique then that Amazon was awarded a U.S. patent for the technology."

Former Shop.org executive director and e-commerce consultant Scott Silverman sees 1-Click as the genesis of an overarching theme at Amazon. "You see it over and over again when you study what connects shoppers to Amazon," he says. "They make processes seamless and frictionless."

Also in 1997, Amazon announced an IPO and began trading on the NASDAQ exchange, appearing to shift perception among Wall Street big-wigs. The e-commerce powerhouse didn't report an annual net profit until January 2004; defying logic, Wall Street remained patient.

"Amazon's horizon for innovation and disruption is five to 10 years, as compared to some investors who can't see beyond 18 months," says John Rossman, managing director at Alvarez & Marsal, former Amazon executive and author of "The Amazon Way." "The company has always been willing to forgo short-term profits and benefits to create a lasting long-term business grounded in innovation and doing what's right for the customer."

Silverman believes Amazon has changed how Wall Street values a company, though he raises a question: "Do the analysts who follow Amazon perceive it to be a retailer or a technology company?"

That question was raised by investors in 2006 when Amazon launched its cloud computing service, Amazon Web Services. While skeptics saw this extension of the business as a distraction, *Forbes* reported earlier this year that AWS grossed $7.9 billion in 2015.

"It disrupted retail by providing small retailers and numerous startups with the server capacity they needed to compete with the big guys," Goldberg says, effectively democratizing e-commerce.

## Endless Aisle

Amazon made it easier for smaller third-party sellers to dip a toe in e-commerce with Amazon's marketplace. Rossman says he and his former team built "a very transparent and robust merchant integration that put customer trust at the absolute center. Our goal was that a customer buying from a third party had to have a trusted experience and we were willing to do whatever it took to make that happen"—including implementing a mandate that Amazon manage the payments and wallet.

Sucharita Mulpuru, former vice president and principal analyst with Forrester Research, also calls the Marketplace disruptive. "It changes how one thinks about the economics of the retail business," she says. "Retail was historically about buying product, marking it up and selling at a profit. Amazon sells product that other people own and they're making very significant, rich margins that they use to subsidize various approaches to customer retention."

Several aspects of selling were controversial when first introduced nearly two decades ago, but some are commonplace today. Two standouts: Selling used books next to new and allowing shoppers to search inside the book.

"Other than cars, no one had ever seen this done before, and here was Amazon allowing the customer to see this on a single detail page," Rossman says. "Publishers and authors didn't like it—obviously they don't make more money on used book sales."

Search inside the book was considered by publishers and authors to be counterintuitive. "Amazon's hypothesis was that if customers got a peek at a few pages, they would actually buy more," he says. "Their intuition was right. The technology became the digital proxy for shopping for a book in a traditional store."

Another fundamental game changer is Amazon's breadth of assortment. "At a time when the megastores like Barnes & Noble and Borders were winning on assortment, along comes Amazon with a million SKUs," Goldberg says, "and those guys watched their competitive advantage slip away."

Experts also deem free shipping noteworthy. Initially, shoppers had to meet thresholds—$75, then $50, then $25. "Marketing expenses became fungible with free shipping," says Ken Seiff, founder and managing partner of Beanstalk Ventures. "It was just genius on Amazon's part."

Seiff calls out the unconventional return policies applied to select items. "They simply tell shoppers to keep some items, as it's cheaper to not pay to ship it back," he says. "It earns them a lot of good will."

Dynamic pricing really changed things, turning retail pricing "into a tech play with … algorithmic pricing rules that allowed for multiple price changes intra-day and inter-day," says Jenn Markey, vice president of marketing at 360pi. "They want to be perceived as a price leader but, in effect, they're using technology to be the fastest follower of the price leader."

She says Amazon created a price leadership position which "brought an unparalleled level of transparency. They also reinforced the concept of a national price" rather than the regional pricing that was more prevalent at the time.

"Shoppers trust Amazon pricing will be the same, regardless of where they live."

## One to One

It's impossible to overlook how Amazon shaped customer buying with the development and expansion of processes such as automated emails, user-generated ratings and reviews and recommendations based on previous purchases.

"There's no substitute for using event-based communication to anticipate and eliminate customer questions and uncertainty, and Amazon understands that better than anyone," Seiff says. "The minute you click to purchase they send an email. Your order ships, they send an email. When the delivery is scheduled, another email lands. This sort of automated communication was game-changing in the direct-to-consumer space."

Several experts believe that Amazon is responsible for creating greater transparency around user-generated content. Though manufacturers initially pressured Amazon not to include ratings and reviews, having them available builds consumer trust.

Scot Wingo, executive chairman and co-founder of ChannelAdvisor, believes the recommendations engine began with books. "It can be difficult to get people to cross categories," he says. It "became a clever way of telling folks, 'If you like this book you might like this movie.' Amazon's growth would not have happened as fast without recommendations."

An unproven membership/loyalty program that met with fierce skepticism when it was introduced in 2005, Amazon Prime now boasts tens of millions of members around the globe.

"It's become the ultimate loyalty program, bundling trust and service," Seiff says. "What they have done with Prime is extraordinary when you realize that for so many Americans, using Prime has become a default behavior."

Amazon Prime Now takes it a giant step further, providing same-day delivery to dozens of metropolitan areas—getting some products into consumers' hands in an hour or less.

"The real disrupter here is the delivery system," Wingo says. "Amazon has created Flex, which is an Uber-like system of independent drivers. With this growing army of shared economy drivers, they can now reach one of four Americans in an hour or less."

## Speed Leads

Amazon builds its logistics infrastructure to support super-fast delivery. In the last 12 months the company has invested in thousands of trailer trucks, moved into ocean shipping, partnered with Atlas Air Worldwide for cargo services and last month debuted Amazon One, its first branded cargo plane.

The company is expanding its footprint of fulfillment centers, moving products ever closer to the consumer and using these vast distribution centers to disrupt fulfillment speeds.

"I'd estimate that they have somewhere around 75 fulfillment centers in the U.S.," Wingo says. "The buildout is nothing short of massive." The first, located near Seattle, was 250,000 square feet. Midwest fulfillment centers tend to be about 1 million square feet; in Texas that bumps to 1.2 million—roughly equivalent to 22 football fields.

Inside fulfillment centers is yet another disrupter, Amazon robotics. At last report Amazon is using over 30,000 robots, including Kiva robots (acquired back in 2012), intelligent forklifts and machines capable of counting items on a shelf. "Amazon continues to invest heavily in robotics in the quest to take humans—and the problems associated with them—out of the equation," Wingo says.

The idea that Amazon is a hybrid retailer/technology provider is repeatedly floated in discussions about the company's role as disrupter. Case in point: Amazon devices.

"There were a few notable things about the Kindle that were revolutionary at the time," Mulpuru says. "It had embedded Internet connectivity so users didn't need to pay extra to buy a book. That completely reduced any friction tied to buying digital goods."

Some washing machine manufacturers have announced plans to build a Dash button-type of interface into the appliance that would reorder detergent; similar technology is already available from Brita. Then there's Amazon Echo, a voice-enabled wireless speaker. This device pushes the envelope on conversation commerce, but it's more than that. Users can request music be played, order pizza, and add products to an Amazon.com shopping cart—all via voice command.

## Eyeing the Future

Perpetually focused on shortening the last mile, Amazon is investing heavily in drones.

"I think we will see it first as a business-to-business thing," Wingo says, "because that is a less complicated path for now." Amazon has already begun drone testing in the United Kingdom, and has introduced Amazon Prime Air, guaranteeing package delivery in 30 minutes or less.

Wingo points out that when Bezos first mentioned the prospect of drone delivery in a 2013 "60 Minutes" interview, Bezos had been investing in it for some time—once again putting Amazon several years ahead of competitors.

## Amazon Is Considering Drone-Friendly Floating Warehouses

[Amazon] has been awarded a patent that describes a logistics technology it calls "airborne fulfillment center (AFC)." The AFC is essentially in airship that's capable of flying at altitudes of 45,000 feet or more that would house items the company sells through its online marketplace. In the patent, Amazon describes a method by which drones would fly into the warehouse, pick up the items they need to deliver, and then deliver those items to the customer's home.

The potential pitfall with drones, however, is that they can only travel so far, so Amazon would technically need to erect a large number of warehouses around the world just to accommodate customers in disparate areas. But rather than look to the ground for fulfillment centers, Amazon is apparently looking to the sky. Like their grounded alternatives, the AFCs would be home to an inventory of items Amazon sells through its online marketplace, according to the patent. New items would be added to the AFC with help from a logistics shuttle that would carry products to and from the device. When an order is placed, a drone would be outfitted with the desired products and descend from the airship. It would then deliver the items to the customer.

*"Amazon Is Considering Drone-Friendly Floating Warehouses," Don Reisinger,*
*Fortune.com, December 29, 2016.*

Less than a year ago Amazon opened its first physical store. "Their stores are innovative in that they turn traditional methods upside down. For most retailers their stores are considered primary touchpoints and the brand's extension online is perceived more like an endless shelf," Wingo says.

"All the arrows flow in the opposite direction. Amazon's physical stores feature online book reviews as part of the display," he says. "Even the pricing approach is an offshoot of the online store. Nothing in Amazon's store has a price. You have to check it with a smartphone because today's retail world is no longer about everyday low prices—it's about prices that change every millisecond." In a word, disruption.

# The Sharing Economy Fosters Innovation

*Lawrence H. Summers and Sarah Cannon*

*In the following viewpoint, Lawrence H. Summers and Sarah Cannon lay out suggestions for how sharing economy firms—those, like Uber and Airbnb, that give people a platform to exchange goods and services person-to-person—and local governments can collaborate to create a regulatory atmosphere that fosters innovation without undermining public trust. Summers served as secretary of the treasury under President Bill Clinton and as director of the White House National Economic Council under President Barack Obama. He is currently the Charles W. Eliot university professor and president emeritus at Harvard University. Cannon, a graduate of Harvard Business School and the Harvard Kennedy School of Government, is vice president of Alphabet's growth equity fund and a team member at the Council on Foreign Relations.*

As you read, consider the following questions:

1. What is the sharing economy business model?
2. Rather than as a "transportation network company," how would Uber like to be classified by regulators?
3. What "positive spillover" do the authors attribute to Airbnb? Can you think of another example?

"How Uber and the Sharing Economy Can Win Over Regulators," by Lawrence H. Summers and Sarah Cannon, Harvard Business School Publishing, October 13, 2014. Reprinted by permission.

S haring economy firms are disrupting traditional industries across the globe. For proof, look no further than Airbnb which, at $10 billion, can boast a higher valuation than the Hyatt hotel chain. Uber is currently valued at $18.2 billion relative to Hertz at $12.5 billion and Avis at $5.2 billion. Beyond individual firms, there are now more than 1,000 cities across four continents where people can share cars. The global sharing economy market was valued at $26 billion in 2013 and some predict it will grow to become a $110 billion revenue market in the coming years, making it larger than the U.S. chain restaurant industry. The revenue flowing through the sharing economy directly into people's wallets will surpass $3.5 billion this year, with growth exceeding 25%, according to Forbes. The business model—where peers can offer and purchase goods and services from each other through an online platform—continues to be applied to new industries from car sharing to peer-to-peer fashion, among many others.

These firms bring significant economic, environmental, and entrepreneurial benefits including an increase in employment and a reduction in carbon dioxide emissions (in the case of car sharing services). Shervin Pishevar, a venture capitalist and an investor in Couchsurfing, Getaround, Uber and other startups in this space, believes these services will have a major impact on the economics of cities; "This is a movement as important as when the web browser came out."

However, rather than rolling out the red carpet, city governments have resisted many of these new entrants issuing subpoenas and cease-and-desist orders. Just in the last month, Pennsylvania's Public Utility Commission issued a cease-and-desist order on Lyft and Uber operations. The companies face fines of $1,000 per day, and 23 drivers face civil and criminal charges.

Regulation is often the most significant barrier to future growth for sharing economy firms. This is particularly unfortunate since the incentives of city governments and sharing economy firms are often aligned. Given the benefits these types of firms bring to cities and firms' vested interest in the very consumer protections that city governments are seeking to ensure, one would expect a less rocky start for these new entrants.

The relationship between sharing economy firms and regulators will likely remain uneasy for the foreseeable future. But companies in this space can benefit from being more cooperative with regulators. As a manager in a sharing economy firm, you can increase the growth of your firm, reduce unnecessary delays, avoid conflict with regulators and expand access for consumers, by pursuing the following maxims:

## Be offensive (rather than defensive) with regulators

The sharing economy is a new concept and many city regulators are unfamiliar with the business model. As a result they are often skeptical and assume sharing economy firms are trying to make a profit by skirting the regulations "traditional" industries (i.e., taxis) face. It makes far more sense to be proactive and explain your business to regulators rather than wait for them to approach you with a concern. By approaching regulators yourself you can avoid misperceptions. It is likely in your interest to reach out to the regulators to explain your business and work with them early on to classify your business under the city's existing regulatory infrastructure rather than having them come to you.

For example, Uber would like to be classified as a communications platform rather than a "transportation network company" and reaching out to local regulators could avoid challenges and conflicts down the road given the nature of the initial classification. Further, given the newness of the business model, regulators may not be aware of how existing regulation may unfairly bias one business model over another, particularly when comparing traditional and sharing economy businesses. For example, rules (currently under consideration in Washington D.C.) that prevent passengers using taxi services from specifying their destination in an effort to avoid discrimination would likely favor

Uber and Lyft over Sidecar (which asks for your destination to facilitate true ridesharing). Firms should not hesitate to pro-actively make the case for fair policy to the relevant regulator.

Lastly, many sharing economy firms are true intermediaries, providing a platform for consumers rather than providing services directly, and should be regulated as such. Without explaining the nature of your firm you will likely be regulated as a traditional firm not as an intermediary resulting in higher taxes and requirements.

## Be responsive to regulators' legitimate concerns

Many sharing economy business models do raise legitimate concerns about user safety, privacy and access. Airbnb needs to be sure the apartments they list are safe for renters and Lyft needs to make sure the cars its drivers use are safe for passengers. Where regulators' concerns are legitimate companies should respond, both because it is the right thing to do and because it will build credibility with the authorities. In making their case, companies should make arguments they would believe if they were regulators.

While it is easy to categorize business as in line with the free market and progressives as anti-market, the reality is far more nuanced. In fact it was a truly bipartisan coalition that drove the de-regulation of the trucking and airline industries in the 1970s. By being focused on consumer interest and responding to regulators legitimate concerns, sharing economy firms will reach a broader audience of advocates than they anticipated and better outcomes.

## Use state of the art approaches to reaching out to government

Just as there are best practices in compensation or writing code, there are best practices in influencing public policy. Best practices in approaching government include, forming coalitions and industry associations to represent a shared point of view rather than each company approaching regulators independently and only in times of crisis. Further, sharing economy firms should seek outside validators. As President Lincoln once said about lawyers, "He who represents himself has a fool for a client." This is even more true in the public relations sphere. Public officials are suspicious of self-interested argumentation and wherever possible it is best to use trusted external validators that can provide a credibility signal that government officials can trust.

## Share your data

Data need not be made public in order to share it with government, and can help your case by reducing regulator concerns. Sharing economy entrepreneur Shelby Clark, founder of car-sharing service RelayRides, suggested the idea of metrics-based regulations. Under this model a firm such as RelayRides could share accident and insurance claim data that could lead to lower insurance requirements given a track record of infrequent accidents. Regulators, like the California Public Utilities Commission, need data to make sure ridesharing firms, for example, aren't restricting access for people in particular neighborhoods or for the disabled. Sharing that data will likely ease these concerns for regulators and minimize requirements for firms. Sharing data about the number of users, for example, enables cities to see the benefits your firm is providing to their citizens in terms of increased transportation options.

## Make a well-researched case for the value provided by your firm

Rather than relying on maxims about the usefulness of the sharing economy, it helps to have concrete data, especially in the face of skeptical regulators. Airbnb commissioned a study that found that; "Because an Airbnb rental tends to be cheaper than a hotel, people stay longer and spent $1,100 in the city, compared with $840 for hotel guests; 14% of their customers said they would not have visited the city at all without Airbnb." These positive spillover effects are a compelling case for authorities in cities like San Francisco, the focus of the study. Although such research is inexpensive since much of it is already gathered by sharing

## Pittsburgh has finally realized it's in a toxic relationship with Uber

Pittsburgh has put up with Uber for a long time. The city stayed quiet as Uber gutted Carnegie Mellon for robotics talent in early 2015, and welcomed the Advanced Technologies Center it later set up. Pittsburgh wrote a letter in support of Uber when the company was fined $11.4 million for operating in Pennsylvania without permission. And in September, Pittsburgh opened its streets to tests of self-driving cars with real people, and played along with Uber's hasty and elaborate press event.

From Uber, Pittsburgh wanted help winning the 2016 Smart City Challenge, a US Department of Transportation competition with a $50 million prize. In May 2016, Peduto asked Uber to spend $25 million on a new transit connection from Carnegie Mellon to the neighborhood where it would be testing autonomous vehicles. Uber not only refused, but came back with a laundry list of things that Pittsburgh could do to better accommodate Uber, among them access to bus lanes, designated pick-up and drop-off spots for self-driving cars, and "prioritization of snow removal" on self-driving car routes. "I would be voted out of office," Peduto retorted at the time. "You aren't offering anything back to the public."

Just five short months ago, Pittsburgh was still positive on its new relationship. When Peduto spoke to Quartz in September, he was optimistic about what Pittsburgh could gain from Uber: data to improve its smart traffic lights, additional services for its senior citizens and commuters with disabilities, substantial job growth if Uber moved any of its vehicle-manufacturing processes to the city. But today Pittsburgh has none of those things, and Uber's biggest show of affection remains a $10,000 donation to a local women's shelter.

*"Pittsburgh has finally realized it's in a toxic relationship with Uber," Alison Griswold, Quartz, February 7, 2017.*

economy firms, it is worth noting that supportive research may already exist, such as an analysis from Susan Shaheen, an expert from U.C. Berkeley, that found that, "car sharers report reducing their vehicle miles travelled by 44% (addressing travel congestion). In addition, surveys in Europe show $CO_2$ emissions are being cut by up to 50%." Firms should marshal such evidence and take it on themselves to publicize the benefits their firms provide.

## Find the best regulations out there and share them with the government

City governments are often under-resourced and many existing rules are simply outdated and are not relevant given the business model of sharing economy firms. There's no reason firms themselves cannot find the best rules out there and propose them to the Mayor's office. It is a challenge for many cities to develop new regulations, and firms could take the first step to gather input from users and consumers to understand existing obstacles and identify outdated rules that need to be re-written in line with these new models. The California Public Utilities Commission decided that 16-point vehicle inspections were required in addition to background checks for drivers for ridesharing services, but a firm like Getaround could just as easily have proposed such a solution. Certainly city governments will make the final decision and firms should not be writing their own regulations, but if there are good rules out there, let the city know.

It is easy to blame regulators for business problems and be right. It is more difficult but far more rewarding to avoid regulatory problems and enjoy business success. Since many of these businesses come out of Silicon Valley it is easy to think the largest risk is the underlying technology or competition. However, the major risk to the viability of many sharing economy firms is that a city or state government rules its business model impermissible. Hoping regulators play along is not an option, and antagonizing city governments is ill-advised. Instead, these firms need to find a new way to do business and should start by sharing with regulators.

# Tech Giants Are Turning Us into Tech Serfs

*Martin Moore*

*In the following viewpoint, Martin Moore argues that digital domination is upon us and that, for better or for worse, its influence is entrenched in our society. But that doesn't mean we must let the tech giants dictate how we live. The policy responses of most governments have been lacking. Reactions seem to be either state control or free market monopoly. But there are surely other alternatives, Moore believes, if only government leaders knew how to look for them. One step is to allow greater competition so that the dominant players in the tech industry do not hold all the cards. Can governments and nonprofits offer public service alternatives? Moore is director of Media Standards Trust, a London-based independent nonprofit news organization that fosters quality, transparency, and accountability for the digital age.*

As you read, consider the following questions:

1. What social media platform does the author credit with motivating voters in 2010?
2. What reason does the author cite for democratic governments becoming anxious about tech giants' reach?
3. What does the author believe governments should do to respond to tech giants?

On 6 May 2010, more than half a million Facebook users voted in the UK election. We know this because they told us. Each of them pressed a button on their Facebook profile announcing they had exercised their electoral right. Their Facebook announcements almost certainly galvanised other people to vote and increased turnout. At least, we know that is what happened in the US election that November. Research on the US Facebook election experiment concluded that the "I voted" button motivated 60,000 voters to go to the polls in the US in 2010, and that in turn triggered 340,000 extra votes. Facebook's intervention took it beyond a passive platform and towards having a more active civic role, but given the decline in voter turnout in the UK and US, few would argue that getting out the vote was not a civic good.

Facebook and other US digital media giants—Google, Twitter, Apple, Amazon and others—have already become integral across our work and social lives. Half of the people in Britain who use the internet are active Facebook users. Google has an 88 per cent share of search in the UK, and 92 per cent in Europe—and even higher in mobile search. Government ministers and departments now rely on Twitter to communicate policy. Eight out of ten ebooks sold in the UK are sold by Amazon.

Many of us rely on these digital behemoths to deliver and store our correspondence, to report our news, to help us find information, to tell us how to get somewhere, to arrange our meetings, to produce and store our work. Nor is our reliance restricted to our social and working lives. Increasingly we are also using these services for democratic purposes. We start and join campaigns on Facebook. We demonstrate political support through Twitter: #jesuischarlie, #bringbackourgirls, #99percent, #icantbreathe. Google accounts for between a quarter and a half of Europeans' method of accessing news online.

One of the consequences of this is that these commercial corporations know an awful lot about us. Facebook is, according to recent academic research, more likely to know what you like than your mum or dad. Apple, on whose iOS platform half of UK smartphone users rely, knows who you call, where you go, and a good proportion of the news you see. As for Google's Android, which now supports the majority of smartphones in the world, the "operating system has only one core function, which is to collect data about you."

This puts a lot of the power over British citizens in the hands of these US media giants. The power to provide or obscure information. The power to assemble and make accessible our digital identities. The power to enable us to connect and co-ordinate with one another. The power—in certain situations—to predict what we are going to do next. And the power to pass on—or sell—our private information, to retailers, media outlets, the security services, or to use for their own purposes. So powerful is the personal data held by these companies that David Cameron put gaining access to it at the forefront of his agenda when he went to see the US president in January.

Yet the UK is just one of many franchises as far as these global titans are concerned. Facebook's 33 million British monthly users make up less than 3 per cent of worldwide Facebook users. This proportion will shrink further if Facebook's ambition to connect some of the four billion unconnected people in the world via internet.org succeeds. The 18 million Britons who rely on Google's Android make up less than 2 per cent of Android users worldwide.

Outside the UK, these US companies' political influence has been even more material and profound. Facebook did not cause the 2011 Egyptian revolution, but it was critical in its incubation and early co-ordination. Twitter did not find Osama bin Laden, but we knew the Americans had thanks to Twitter. Amazon did successfully (though only temporarily) shut down access to Wikileaks when it dropped it from its cloud.

Until the last couple of years most democratic countries have simply stood by and watched as these global behemoths have grown. We have been happy to be gifted their digital tools that make our lives more efficient, more connected and—digitally, at least—more transparent.

Only recently have democratic governments begun to get anxious. It is not surprising that they are worried. These companies dominate markets and in some areas monopolise them. Some of these services are arguably becoming utilities, deprived of whose benefits one becomes unable to participate fully in society.

Moreover, they have increased their penetration and their scope far beyond the private sphere. Microsoft has developed predictive policing software. Amazon Web Services runs the CIA's data cloud. Google predicts the spread of flu. Facebook promotes voting in elections and helps find missing children. Yet they are almost all US companies, and often do not have their headquarters in the countries in which they operate. Most have located their European offices in tax-friendly Ireland or Luxembourg.

The UK government, and UK citizens, have very little influence over these tech giants, or how they behave. We trust they will be kind and do no evil, but have little leverage if they choose to do otherwise. As Rebecca MacKinnon wrote of Facebook and Google+, the two "share a Hobbesian approach to governance in which people agree to relinquish a certain amount of freedom to a benevolent sovereign who in turn provides security and other services."

The recent Intelligent Services Committee report on the murder of Lee Rigby lamented the UK government's lack of power. "None of the US companies we contacted," the report says, "accept the UK's jurisdiction on requests for Lawful Intercept (i.e. content) for intelligence investigations." These US companies included Facebook, Google, BlackBerry, Microsoft, Yahoo, Apple and Twitter. Given the increasing use of encryption, the report goes on: "[W]e consider this to be the single most important challenge that the [UK Security] Agencies face. It has very serious ramifications for the security of the UK."

Non-democratic states have already taken steps to neuter these digital giants. Some have sought to block or constrain them, while nurturing national—and more compliant—alternatives. China blocked Facebook in 2009 (though, after assiduous courting by

Mark Zuckerberg, is considering letting it back in). Google operates in China, but its service is frequently disrupted, meaning its share languishes at less than 2 per cent. Russia has gone further, with its lower House passing legislation in 2014 that would require internet companies to store Russian citizens personal data within Russia. Combined with the RuNet website blacklist, the restrictions on blogs with a daily audience of more than 3,000, and the "law against retweets," this means the Russian government will have huge power over its citizens' digital behavior, and have full knowledge of its citizens' digital footprints.

Erich Honecker's East German government could only dream of having this much information about and control over its citizens. No democratic state should want to go in this direction—or, if they do, then they would quickly lose any democratic credibility.

So how should the UK and other democratic societies respond? What are the alternatives to blithely accepting US digital dominance or reacting in an autocratic anti-democratic way? Have Europe's responses to date been well-informed, forward-thinking, constructive and cognizant of civil liberties? Sadly not.

In November 2014 the EU Parliament proposed breaking up Google into separate parts—splitting search from maps, news, email and social. Even though this was a symbolic gesture it is not clear why the Parliament thought such a move would be constructive. The chief alternatives to Google in search, maps, "free" email and social are also all US tech giants.

Two months earlier George Osborne announced, with some fanfare, that "some technology companies go to extraordinary lengths to pay little or no tax here … My message to those companies is clear: we will put a stop to it." Yet, as numerous commentators subsequently concluded, the new tax arrangements are unlikely to have much impact beyond sending a political message to Google and its peers.

The November 2014 UK government report into the killing of Lee Rigby proposed, amongst other things, that Facebook and others keep their users under surveillance and pass on information to the UK government. Not only is this technologically impractical (there are 4.75 billion pieces of content shared a day on Facebook), but creates a dangerous precedent. This would essentially mean Facebook acting as a sort of private sector GCHQ, scouring people's profiles and correspondence for any evidence of potential terrorism or criminality (and note the ambiguity "potential").

Perhaps the most regressive proposal of all was David Cameron's promise, in January 2015, that, should the Conservatives be re-elected, he would pass laws to ensure that there were no "safe spaces" online where people could communicate without the government being able to gain access. Not only would this be technically impossible, to head in this direction would take the UK on a path pursued by authoritarian statist countries like Russia and China.

Cameron's proposal, and others across Europe, indicate a wider policy vacuum. There is a digital policy black hole regarding how to deal with these companies into which regressive, reactive policies are being proposed without much thought for their practical application or their negative implications. As yet there are almost no proposed democratic alternatives. We have no separate, plausible, social-democratic option as distinct from the US free market individualist model or authoritarian statism.

This is because there has, to date, been so little substantive policy thinking about how to respond to these digital giants in a way that both acknowledges and welcomes the significant benefits they bring, but also enables us—over time—to create an environment in which we no longer rely on them so much.

If we want greater competition in the search market, why have we not discussed how to make the web easier to navigate (for example through more consistent metadata)? If we are concerned about tech giants hoarding personal data, why not consider Evgeny Morozov's suggestion that such data "stripped of privacy-compromising identifiers... be pooled into a common resource"? If Twitter—which has always struggled to make a profit—closed down tomorrow, would we simply do without it, or wait for the market to come up with an alternative? Should we consider whether the BBC could build a public service alternative—building in proper safeguards for independence and privacy protection? If we are genuinely concerned about misuse of our private data by these US firms, should we not explore the "information fiduciary" concept suggested by Jack Balkin and others?

Our failure to explore alternatives may be due to our inability to foresee the dangers. The usefulness and convenience of these digital tools makes us blind to the potential economic, social and political risks. Until these dangers become clearer then there will be little political will to take action.

Meanwhile, our reliance on these digital leviathans continues to grow. Within the last year both Facebook and Google have taken significant steps into the world of work (see Facebook @ work and Google MyBusiness) and expanded into new markets (such as through Facebook's internet.org). If, at some point in the near future, there is another terrorist attack in the UK, the government will again place some blame on these US corporations and try to respond. Deprived of constructive, intellectually robust responses it is highly likely they will react in a way that harms not just the companies themselves, but all of us who have come to rely on them for our work, our social life and—increasingly—our civic participation.

On 7 May, many of us may click on a new Facebook "I voted" button. This will encourage more of us to vote. Facebook will have performed a civic good. But, as Jonathan Zittrain pointed out with respect to the 2010 election experiment, there is nothing to stop Facebook deliberately prompting only certain voters and thereby skewing the result. How would we ever know? Even if we did know, or found out, there is nothing we could do about it. As these tech giants bring us unprecedented tools for civic participation, we have a responsibility to think more carefully about how to ensure they "don't be evil."

## Periodical and Internet Sources Bibliography

*The following articles have been selected to supplement the diverse views presented in this chapter.*

Marc Andreessen, "Why Software Is Eating the World," *Wall Street Journal,* August 20, 2011. https://www.wsj.com/articles/SB100014 24053111903480904576512250915629460.

Franklin Foer, "Amazon Must Be Stopped," *New Republic,* October 9, 2014. https://newrepublic.com/article/119769/amazons -monopoly-must-be-broken-radical-plan-tech-giant.

Paul Ford, "What Is Code?" *Bloomberg Businessweek,* June 11, 2015. https://www.bloomberg.com/graphics/2015-paul-ford-what-is -code.

Joi Ito, Scott Dadich, and President Barack Obama, "Barack Obama, Neural Nets, Self-Driving Cars, and the Future of the World," October 2016. https://www.wired.com/2016/10/president -obama-mit-joi-ito-interview.

Jill Lepore, "The Disruption Machine," *New Yorker,* June 23, 2014. http://www.newyorker.com/magazine/2014/06/23/the -disruption-machine.

Kevin Maney, "How Artificial Intelligence and Robots Will Radically Transform the Economy," *Newsweek,* November 30, 2016. http:// www.newsweek.com/2016/12/09/robot-economy-artificial -intelligence-jobs-happy-ending-526467.html.

Jack Nicas, "Silicon Valley Stumbles in World Beyond Software," *Wall Street Jorunal,* December 6, 2016. https://www.wsj.com/articles /silicon-valley-stumbles-in-world-beyond-software-1481042474.

Noam Scheiber, "The Brutal Ageism of Tech," *New Republic,* March 23, 2014. https://newrepublic.com/article/117088/silicons -valleys-brutal-ageism.

Lauren Smiley, "The Shut-In Economy," *Matter,* March 23, 2015, https://medium.com/matter/the-shut-in-economy- ec3ec1294816#.j13w2f8b1

Anna Wiener, "Uncanny Valley," *N+1,* Spring 2016. https:// nplusonemag.com/issue-25/on-the-fringe/uncanny-valley.

**GLOBAL**VIEWPOINTS

# CHAPTER 2

# Technology's Mark on Our World

# Privacy May Be a Price We Have to Pay

*Paul Levy*

*In the following viewpoint, Paul Levy argues that the privacy policies issued by the biggest tech companies do not actually reflect much in the way of protection. Instead, user privacy is sold and traded like a commodity. Most users and consumers seem to accept the loss of privacy in exchange for free services or exciting innovation. Whether that is a result of apathy, naivete, or a sophisticated understanding of our brave new world is unknown. Levy predicts that privacy will become an issue of greater concern in the future, but the challenge will be to disrupt the status quo. Levy is senior researcher in innovation management at University of Brighton and the author of* Digital Inferno.

As you read, consider the following questions:

1. What piece of technology does the author use to engage the reader with his concerns about privacy?
2. What does the term "disruptive technology" refer to?
3. What did Edward Snowden say is one of Google's biggest allies in the privacy war?

"Privacy Is Fast Becoming the Real Disruptive Force in Digital Technology," by Paul Levy, The Conversation, February 11, 2015. https://theconversation.com/privacy-is-fast-becoming-the-real-disruptive-force-in-digital-technology-37244. Licensed under CC BY-ND 4.0 International.

D id you recently buy a Samsung smart TV? If you are worried about privacy, you may be wondering how smart that decision was following the manufacturer's warnings that its voice-activated televisions may record personal information—that is, your conversations—and transmit them to a third party.

The voice-activated television monitors spoken conversations to listen for commands and transmits them to another firm which performs the voice analysis. Samsung stated that the televisions may even do so when the voice-activation feature is turned off.

Such privacy snafus seem to be the norm these days: only recently Google, following a UK Information Commissioner's Office ruling, agreed to rewrite its privacy policy to make it "more accessible" and "to allow users to find its controls more easily" and, most pertinently, for its privacy policy to comply with the UK Data Protection Act. The Netherlands, too, threatened Google with a £12m fine if it didn't put its affairs in order.

Facebook had to take similar steps in 2014, yet the changes do not fundamentally improve privacy, but simply ensure that the way our privacy is treated is easier to understand—especially where our data is part of a business model based on targeted advertising. Simply put, when we sign up, we still agree to share our data.

## An Open-Door Approach to Data

Most of the changes to Google's privacy policy concern clearly informing users how their information will be treated. The default setting for users will still be allow the use of their data unless they specifically opt out. Getting this data out of you and passing it around is the deal users make in exchange for free, advertising-based web services.

But it's endlessly apparent how firms that are evangelical about the need for user data to be accessible to them are nevertheless vague about how they then use it. Terms and conditions are long and bamboozling. The Information Commissioner described Google's guidelines on privacy as "baffling." And Google isn't acting proactively, but dragging its feet until the regulator demands action.

# Mobile Data Access in Developing Nations

You've probably never heard of Jana, but for millions in the developing world it's a meal ticket to the mobile Web. Indian users of its mCent app can get 13 rupees' worth of mobile data as a reward for downloading and trying LINE, a chat app, or 28 rupees' worth for using the music service Saavn, free data they can use to surf the Web or look for a job.

LINE and Saavn pay for the data, and Jana takes a cut. Its goal beyond increasing profits is to provide free Internet to billions of people. Fanciful as that sounds, mCent has collected 30 million users in less than a year, thanks to long-standing partnerships with 311 mobile operators in 93 countries.

Mobile data costs up to 10% of a person's average wage in Brazil, Eagle says, and more than a third of someone's income in Africa, while in the U.S. it's more like 1% to 2%, according to the ITU.

The result: Only 57% of India's smartphone owners bother turning on their data, and those who do consume a mere 80MB per month on average, about a tenth of what Americans use.

Google's Project Loon and Facebook's Internet.org both include plans to beam free Wi-Fi over developing nations from high-altitude balloons or drones, but test flights are only recently ramping up, and it'll likely be years before there's any real-world impact.

*"This App Is Cashing In on Giving the World Free Data," by Parmy Olson,* Forbes, *July 29, 2015.*

Facebook's apparently easier-to-read and more accessible privacy policy now permits data to pass between Facebook, WhatsApp and Instagram—an approach that has brought the scrutiny of German and Dutch data regulators. Facebook's reasoning is that we'll see adverts that are more relevant—the company is only trying to help. Yet consumer concerns remain, largely because the pace of change and this transition to a default of openness has arrived so quickly. When people find out what happens to their data, many are shocked at what they've signed up to.

So, what is really going on here, and what should we be concerned about?

## Privacy Is a Disruptive Technology

The term disruptive technology is often found alongside terms such as 3D printing, robotics, or artificial intelligence. According to the Harvard Business Review:

> Disruptive technologies introduce a very different package of attributes from those mainstream customers historically value, and they often perform far worse along one or two dimensions that are particularly important to those customers... At first, then, disruptive technologies tend to be used and valued only in new markets or new applications.

Data harvesting, data mining and analysis has transformed the way we look at our mobile devices and computer screens. Content is now adaptive and responsive to our behaviour. But that does not necessarily mean that these are technologies many of us want or need.

Our online communication tools such as email and social media, largely free at point of use, are based upon optimising revenue through targeted advertising. For this to be cost-effective, the underlying technology was required to be disruptive—both in the way we socially interact and in its capacity to deliver commercial value. We have all noticed how social media has fundamentally disrupted our lives, but until fairly recently the underlying systems and software that can unravel who we are and what we are doing, and share this data in order to influence our consumer behaviour, have been paid little attention.

Not everyone is against this disruption: as Edward Snowden pointed out in 2013, public indifference is one of Google's biggest allies in the privacy war. So Google's reluctance should come as no surprise, because its current direction is based on disrupting its users' privacy.

As is often the case, one disruptive technology gives rise to another: the dark web is one reaction to the attempt to disrupt our freedom to be private, but the jury is out on whether efforts to reframe the current debate will succeed. The privacy-friendly Facebook competitor, Ello, was given considerable publicity but has already been written-off by many, while the privacy-regarding cloud storage Spideroak seeks to challenge the likes of Google Drive and Dropbox.

But these are just tiny eddies in a river of free-to-use online services which treat user privacy as a saleable, tradeable commodity for corporations.

## Measure and Counter-Measure

So there seems to be a growing battle between corporations and users. Google, Microsoft, Amazon and other firms have been using their muscle to pay firms creating ad-blocking software to stop blocking. I believe this war has only really just begun, with the tweaks to manage privacy—both to strip it away and to protect it—representing a volatile, emerging disruptive force.

Even as Google Glass freaked most users out, the battle for access to our private thoughts and concerns is just getting going. The challenge for those innovating to protect privacy is to come up with viable alternatives that can change the current status quo. In the meantime perhaps you should, be careful what you say in your own living room.

# Combating Online Terrorist Recruitment

*Rami Alhames*

*In the following viewpoint, Rami Alhames notes that social media is the main communication system for terrorist groups like ISIS to recruit new members and distribute extremist propaganda. Tech companies are working together to combat this propaganda machine, but Alhames argues that smaller, independent groups and even individuals can join in the fight. Often the solution is as simple as reporting the user to the host, but some groups work to destroy ISIS-related accounts. But what effect these efforts have had on ISIS is in question, and some experts believe this is one instance where a human approach can have more impact than technology. Alhames is a writer and translater who regularly contributes to Global Voices.*

As you read, consider the following questions:

1. What percentage of foreign recruits to ISIS are from Western Europe?
2. Approximately how many ISIS Twitter accounts were targeted at the writing of this article?
3. What does the MIT Technology Review suggest to curb recruitment?

D espite technological efforts to contain or eliminate their presence on social media, ISIS has amassed substantial power online.

It is difficult to quantify the precise impact of ISIS' efforts to promote its mission and recruit new members. But some data suggest that it is having an impact. According to a 2015 study by King's College London's International Centre for the Study of Radicalisation and Political Violence, "the number of foreigners that have joined Sunni militant organizations in the Syria/Iraq conflict continues to rise." According to ICSR's latest estimate, "the total now exceeds 20,000—of which nearly a fifth were residents or nationals of Western European countries."

Social media platforms have also been in the media spotlight as a key avenue for ISIS to spread its message and recruit new members. Writing for Reuters, security and intelligence expert Rita Katz describes ISIS' use of social media as a unique within the realm of violent extremist organizations' activity:

> Until the rise of Islamic State, extremist activity and exchanges online usually took place inside restricted, password-protected jihadist forums. But Islamic State brought online jihadism out of the shadows and into the mainstream, using social media— especially Twitter—to issue rapid updates on its successes to a theoretically unlimited audience.

Facebook and Twitter have sought to prevent ISIS from marketing its graphic and hate speech content to the masses, but balancing these efforts with their commitments to free expression is no small feat. On Wired, Julia Greenberg writes:

> ...the challenge for sites like Facebook and Twitter goes beyond tracking down content that promotes terrorism. It also requires defining "promoting terrorism." In a sense, the two platforms are global communities, each engaged in a constant process of determining community norms as the use of the platforms evolves.

But another part of the story, one that has garnered far less attention than the efforts of big companies and governments, are the many independent groups and individuals making their own efforts to combat ISIS' activities online.

Twitter account @reportterrorist claims that there are 50K ISIS Twitter accounts it needs to bring down.

Anonymous has published a series of guides to help those seeking to join its "war on ISIS" to track and identify the group's websites. It dedicates Twitter account @TeamDestroyISIS to retweet, mock and hunt down ISIS accounts accompanied by the hashtag #OpISIS.

Several individual Arab netizens have joined the international coalition against ISIS online. One of these contributions is the Twitter account @KSAssa or Saudi Arabia Electronic Army, with 20.7K followers, which is taking the lead to stop and "destroy" accounts related to ISIS and "every enemy" that threatens the country's unification: "Your cooperation and activity is essential to delete the accounts of criminals and vandals, the enemies of religion and our homeland."

There is also @BlockDaesh, lead by @Mujtahid_i (30.4K followers), which aims to bring down ISIS Twitter spam accounts.

Although the account @faaars444 (25K followers) was originally created to ban pro-ISIS accounts that target Saudi national youths to join the group, the account has recently changed its mission. After the political rift between Saudi Arabia and Iran, following Saudi Arabia's execution of top Shia Cleric Nimr Al Nimr, the account converted to fight the "Safadis," the most significant ruling dynasties of Persia in what known today as Iran, or in other words, Shia: "I decided to change the activity from fighting against ISIS, especially these days, to fight the Safadis; and will get back to ISIS, God willing."

And the question yet is beyond the air strikes and on-ground military operations.

But taking down ISIS websites is like shooting fish in a barrel, writes the Fight ISIS blog:

> There is soo many targets out there right now on Twitter, Facebook, YouTube, and Sendvid all are flooded with ISIS users and Propaganda. You can help and you do not even need to be a Hacker to Shut Down ISIS Web Sites !!
>
> Most of the Web sites, all we have to do is report the User to the Host (like twitter, facebook, Etc.) and they will Suspend or Shutdown the User / ISIS account.

The MIT Technology Review proposed a more human approach, arguing that what's missing is direct contact with the young generation (Muslims or non-Muslims) who are being targeted by ISIS to disprove jihadist propaganda:

> Indeed, the technological response to stanching the recruitment isn't having much of an effect. Internet companies close accounts and delete gory videos; they share information with law enforcement. Government agencies tweet out countermessages and fund general outreach efforts in Muslim communities. Various NGOs train religious and community leaders in how to rebut ISIS messaging, and they create websites with peaceful interpretations of the Quran. But what's missing is a widespread effort to establish one-on-one contact online with the people who are absorbing content from ISIS and other extremist groups and becoming radicalized.

# Tech Giants Must Take a Stand for Consumer Protection

*John Thornhill*

*In the following viewpoint, John Thornhill surveys the back-and-forth between Apple and the FBI over an iPhone that belonged to Syed Farook, who opened fire on an office full of people in San Bernardino, California. Although the device belonged to Farook's employer, and the FBI had a warrant to search it, the device was locked by a passcode, so the FBI asked Apple to build a "backdoor"—a bit of software to circumvent the passcode. Apple refused. Such software, it said, would give its possessor the power to ravage encryption, a dangerous precedent. As Thornhill writes, "It is one thing to hand over all accessible data upon receipt of a lawful request; it is quite another to be forced to create a backdoor into its own products." Thornhill is the innovation editor at the* Financial Times.

As you read, consider the following questions:

1. How many requests for device information did Apple receive from the United States government in the first six months of 2015?
2. On what grounds did Apple refuse to comply with the FBI's request that they unlock the San Bernardino shooter's iPhone?
3. What distinction does the author draw between complying with a data request and building a backdoor?

People have long worried about technology invading their lives. The front cover of Newsweek magazine, illustrated by a telephone, camera and tape recorder, once captured those fears, asking: "Is Privacy Dead?" The date: July 1970.

Since then, we have seen the mass introduction of personal devices such as laptop computers, smartphones and health monitors. Today, more than 6bn such devices connected to the internet are being added each day. Most of them are vulnerable to being hacked by those ingenious or devious enough. We truly live in a golden age of surveillance, in which every step we take and every heart flutter we make can be recorded, for better or worse.

Our governments are desperate for us to keep that information secure—but, understandably, they also want selective access to that mass of data when national security demands. The technology companies, which often stand between governments and users, have mostly been happy to comply with lawful requests for such data.

Apple's latest transparency report, covering the first six months of 2015, records that the company received 3,824 requests for device information from US law enforcement authorities. It provided data in 81 per cent of those cases.

The company operates a 24-hour hotline to respond to such requests and promptly helped the police investigate the San Bernardino attacks last year when two Islamist terrorists murdered 14 people. But when the FBI later demanded that Apple write special software to help crack a locked iPhone used by one of the killers, the company resisted, claiming this could jeopardise the security of all iPhone users. The FBI accused the company of obstructing its investigation. A heated row has ended up in court.

This month, the FBI hit the pause button on those legal proceedings, saying it might have found another way of cracking the iPhone. Nevertheless, the case raises important issues of principle and precedent that resonate in all democratic countries trying to balance the demands of security against the rights of privacy. In spite of the odium heaped upon the company, Apple has done the right thing to stress-test these issues in court.

As the Center for Democracy and Technology, a civil rights organisation, has argued in a court submission: "If the government succeeds in this case, the relationship between technology providers and users will be forever altered."

This is not the first time US law enforcement agencies have tried to force Apple to override its security procedures, and on occasion the company has complied. Last year, however, at the invitation of a New York judge, Apple contested such an order in a case involving a drug dealer who subsequently pleaded guilty. In February, that judge ruled in the company's favour.

Even though the New York and San Bernardino cases differ in important respects, the ruling by Judge James Orenstein is worth reading because of the arguments he highlighted.

The issue of principle concerns whether a company can be conscripted by the government into taking actions that it believes endanger its users' rights and its commercial interests. It is one thing to hand over all accessible data upon receipt of a lawful request; it is quite another to be forced to create a backdoor into its own products.

Judging there was a significant legal difference between active obstruction and passive refusal, Mr Orenstein ruled: "Apple is not 'thwarting' anything—it is merely declining to offer assistance." The issue of precedent revolves around whether it is appropriate for the government to use the All Writs Act of 1789 to force Apple to comply with its demands, as it has tried to do in both cases. Mr Orenstein concluded it was not, given that Congress had recently rejected legislation granting such powers.

The judge called for further debate in Congress between legislators who understood the technological realities of a world that their predecessors could not begin to conceive. "It would betray our constitutional heritage and our people's claim to democratic governance for a judge to pretend that our Fathers already had that debate, and ended it, in 1789," he concluded.

Mr Orenstein's ruling is far from the final judgment in the broader debate. The Department of Justice is appealing against his decision. This may all seem a messy process, but it can sometimes prove to be the useful means by which democracies grope towards greater legal clarity.

# Privacy and Free Speech Are Not Mutually Exclusive

*George Brock*

*In the following viewpoint, George Brock examines the question, "Who gets to decide whether free speech or privacy prevails in any given case?" In 2014, the European Court of Justice issued a profound ruling: European citizens have the right to ask search engines to remove links to information they find unflattering. It is known as the "right to be forgotten." Here, Brock argues that as courts, countries, citizens, and corporations reckon with the implications of a vague right, they will have to address the reality that neither privacy nor press freedom are ever absolute. Brock is a professor of journalism at City University London. His latest book is* Out of Print: Newspapers, Journalism, and the Business of News in the Digital Age.

As you read, consider the following questions:

1. Which court rules on the "right to be forgotten"?
2. What is an example of a "preponderant interest" that would prohibit de-indexing?
3. Why does the author believe "privacy and free expression are matters of colliding rights"?

"How 'Right to Be Forgotten' Puts Privacy and Free Speech on a Collision Course," by George Brock, The Conversation Media Group Ltd, November 18, 2016. https://theconversation.com/how-right-to-be-forgotten-puts-privacy-and-free-speech-on-a-collision-course-68997. Licensed Under CC BY-ND 4.0 International.

The age of digital technology, in which we can search and retrieve more information than we could in any previous era, has triggered a debate over whether we have too much information. Is the cure to "unpublish" things we think are wrong or out of date? Ought we have a "right to be forgotten"?

Until recently, this was an argument conducted in Europe and South America and given a powerful push by a decision in 2014 from the European Union's highest court to provide a legally enforceable right to remove some material from internet searches.

Now the issue has reached American newsrooms. The dilemma is simple to describe and painfully hard to solve. People who have had long-ago brushes with the law or bankruptcy would prefer such information not to be at the top of search results on their name. Foolish pranks immortalised on Facebook may be harming someone's chances of getting a job.

American editors are now getting so many requests to erase or unlink online material that they've been consulting pundits and lawyers for help. American media law, based around the First Amendment guaranteeing press freedom, is very different to European law.

But the development of the EU's right to be forgotten is a poor precedent for the US or anywhere else. The European version of the right to be forgotten—really a conditional right to be taken out of internet searches—is carelessly written, based on muddled ideas and contains risks for free expression.

The "right to be forgotten" is an emblematic battle at the new frontier between privacy and freedom—both of speech and the right to know. It is a case study of the dilemmas which we will face. Who gets to decide whether free speech or privacy prevails in any given case? And on what criteria?

## Gonzales' Gripe

In 2009 a Barcelona resident, Mario Costeja Gonzales, complained to Google that a search for his name produced—at the top of the first page—a newspaper item from 1998 which recorded that some of his property had been sold to pay debts. It was given unfair prominence and was out of date said Sr Gonzales. He asked La Vanguardia, the newspaper, to erase the item. Both search engine and newspaper rejected his complaint.

The case went to court. The court ruled out any action against the paper but referred the question of the search link to the EU's Court of Justice. In 2014, the court said that Sr Gonzales did indeed have a right to ask Google to de-index items which would be produced by a search on his name—under certain conditions (and there's a degree of irony that he fought a battle over the right for this small story to be forgotten only to become a global cause célèbre over the issue).

And the conditions are the heart of the matter. Google routinely de-indexes material from search results: copyright infractions (by the million), revenge porn, details of bank accounts or passport numbers. The court said that search results could be incompatible with the EU's data protection directive and must be removed if:

> … that information appears … to be inadequate, irrelevant or no longer relevant, or excessive in relation to the purposes of the processing at issue carried out by the operator of the search engine.

The judges went on to say that, as a rule, the individual's "data" or privacy rights outrank the search engine's commercial interest or the public's right to know. But that would not be the case if the public had a "preponderant interest" in the information—as would be the case if the individual was in public life.

You might say, what could be more natural than this? The internet has unleashed a flood of stuff: we must have some way of protecting ourselves from the obvious harm it can cause. Carefully, transparently and accountably done, it does not have to amount to "censorship"—the claim from many voices when the judgement first appeared.

Google has taken down 1.72 billion URLs after 566,000 requests. Press freedom and free expression were never absolute—we allow some criminal convictions to be forgotten, we have libel and contempt of court laws. All restrain publication.

The problem lies with much data protection law—principally in the EU—which fails to balance the competing rights. The court judgement's tests for whether something ought to be de-indexed are vague and opaque. How do we test for the relevance of information? Relevant to whom? When does information go out of date?

The case wasn't about defamation: no one claimed Sr Gonzales has been libelled. It was not about correcting inaccuracy. It wasn't private: it had been made public quite legally. The court made clear that a successful claim did not have to show that harm or distress has been caused.

## Muddling Through

The intellectual origins of data protection law lie in the traumas of 20th-century Europe. The Dutch government in the 1930s recorded with characteristic thoroughness the details of every one of their citizens: name, age, address and so forth. So when Nazi Germany occupied the Netherlands all they had to do to locate the Jewish and gypsy populations was open the filing cabinets. The secret police of communist states in the second half of the century and their carefully filed surveillance reinforced the lesson that secretly stored data can inflict damage.

The "right to be forgotten" is a muddled solution and fails to clarify a specific remedy for a particular problem. Here are a few of the issues which we are going to have to deal with:

Although the Gonzalez case made the compromise of leaving the online newspaper archive untouched while stopping search engines finding it, we have now had two cases—in Italy and Belgium—where courts have ordered news media archives to be altered.

Google's chief privacy counsel once said that his company is creating new jurisprudence about privacy and free speech. What he didn't say is that Google is doing all this virtually in secret. Its decisions can be challenged in court by a litigant with money and patience, but should a private corporation be doing this at all?

There is a major unsolved problem about how far the right to be forgotten reaches. The French government thinks that it should be global, which is disproportionate as well as unfeasible.

## What's to Be Done?

The market isn't providing ways to protect privacy—and individuals often part with their information barely knowing that they have surrendered some privacy. But the history of free expression has surely taught us that we should be very cautious about restrictions. If you want an alternative to the sweeping tests in EU law, have a look at the stiff tests laid out by the free speech organisation Article 19. Judges in several EU countries—notably the Netherlands—have tightened the tests for allowing material to be delinked.

EU law needs to recognise that privacy and free expression are matters of colliding rights which can't be wished away by pretending that there's no conflict. Collisions of basic rights can't be abolished—they can only be managed.

The Gonzales judgement didn't start the right to be forgotten but it did bring it to the attention of the world. It did some good by correcting thousands of small harms. But because it addressed the rights involved in such a muddled and careless way, it opened up risks to freedom of speech. The judges of the future need to do better.

# We Must Decide If Our Digital Presence Is the Same Nationally as Globally

*Luciano Floridi*

*In the following excerpted viewpoint, Luciano Floridi argues that Google's transnationalism has complicated the implementation of the "right to be forgotten." If Google complies with a request to delink in France, should it also remove that link from google.es (Spain) and google.de (Germany) and, for that matter, any version of Google worldwide? Does the "right to be forgotten" transcend borders? Floridi, responding to a report on the matter issued by Google's advisory council, provides a pragmatic solution while arguing that more needs to be done to ensure successful implementation and progression of the law. Floridi is a professor of philosophy and the ethics of information at the University of Oxford.*

As you read, consider the following questions:

1. What does the author mean when he writes "the power of default is enormous"?
2. What compromise to global delinking does the author support?
3. Why does the author believe that future generations may show less of an instinct for privacy?

---

For centuries, roughly since the Peace of Westphalia (1648), political geography has provided jurisprudence with an easy answer to the question of how far a ruling should apply—that is, as far as the national borders within which the legal authority operates. A bit like "my place, my rules; your place your rules." It may now seem obvious but it took a long time and immense suffering to reach such a simple approach. And it's still perfectly fine today, as long as you operate within a physical space. However, when it comes to the Internet, the space is logical, being made of data, protocols, URLs, interfaces and so forth. Which means that any place is only a click away. The result is that a ruling that concerns the Internet cannot rely on the old, Westphalian solution.

If you ask Google to delink personal information in Spain, all it takes to find the removed links is to check the same search engine in another country. The non-territoriality of the Internet works wonders with the unobstructed circulation of information. In China, for example, the government has to make a constant and sustained effort to control information online. But the same feature proves awkward if you are trying to implement the right to be forgotten.

[…]

Personally, I argued in favor of a more restricted, nation-based delinking. The reasons in favor of this option are pragmatic. Most users never leave their local search engines. Also because of linguistic reasons, Spaniards use google.es, Italians google.it, Germans google.de and so forth. The power of default is enormous.

It follows that if Alice, who is French and lives in Paris, asks Google to delink some legally published information about herself, the most effective implementation is to remove the links from Alice's local search engine, namely google.fr. Over 95 percent of all searches in Europe are on local versions of Google. Thus, it is useless to remove them also from google.pt because virtually nobody in France will ever care to check information about Alice using the Portuguese version of Google, while the very few who may care will not be deterred by a pan-European delinking anyway.

Someone who is determined to find a piece of information about Alice will simply use a search engine not based in Europe. Some have bitten the bullet and argued that all this is correct, but this is precisely why the delinking should be worldwide—that is, applied to all versions of any search engine.

In the case of Google, this means delinking the information in question also from, for example, google.br (Brazil). I disagree. Why? Remember: my place my rules, but your place your rules. How could one explain to Brazilians that some legally published information online should no longer be indexed in a Brazilian search engine because the European Court of Justice has ruled so? Would the opposite also apply? Could Brazilians appeal? And how could one determine what is of public interest in this or that country? Maybe I am an investor from Brazil, and I do need to know whether a person has (for example) had some properties repossessed in the past.

Some have called for Google to extend its delinking to all its global search sites, since they are accessible within Europe. However, consider the following scenario. The day after some worldwide delinking starts being implemented, nothing will stop undemocratic and illiberal places from hosting a search engine that provides links to all information anyway. It would be ironic if we were to find information using a search engine based in North Korea because it was more complete than the local ones. Geographical space is no longer the solution; so the approach recommended by the report is a good compromise that adapts an outdated answer to a new question. It does not work very well but it is the classic "better than nothing" solution. Opting for a global delinking would be, instead, the classic "perfect is the enemy of good." It would be just another way of killing the Westphalian approach by asking the world to adapt to European decisions.

When it came to finalizing the text of the report, I was happy, pragmatically, to concede the point because a pan-European delinking simply adds nothing to a national one, in terms of effective protection of individuals. It would be a different story if one were to argue that some legally published information online should be removed (the information itself, not just the link) altogether or blocked at the source (for example, by not allowing any search engine to index it in the first place). I am not against similar options, but I suspect that, in order to consider them, we would have to have a serious debate about how harmful the information in question needs to be to justify such a drastic solution. But this is something with which not everybody in favor of the "right to be forgotten" seems to be willing to engage.

The second point concerns the publishers, and it is simpler. I am of the view that publishers should be fully involved in the evaluation of a delinking request. They should have the right to know about whether someone has requested a search engine to delink some information that they legally published; to be informed about what decision has been taken by the search engine with regard to such a request; and to appeal, if they disagree with the delinking decision. All this applies even more strongly if a worldwide delinking approach were to be adopted.

Of course, the risk is that, by informing the publishers, one may enable them to re-publish the same contents in ways that can bypass the ruling and the delinking decision itself, both of which concern only personal information and hence "name and surname" searches. Yet this is a case in which I would recommend a principled approach. One could certainly implement disincentives, but the fact that publishers may misuse the meta-information about a delinking request is not an argument against their right to know and hence being able to appeal. This will be even more obvious the further we move towards a situation in which not being indexed by a search engine simply means "not being," full stop. In this case too, the report has found a fair balance, by recommending Google to follow the good practice of notifying the publishers "to the extent allowed by the law." It is a bit vague, and I would have liked to see an even more incisive position in favor of a full involvement of the publishers throughout the process, but it is a satisfactory compromise.

At the end of our consultations and internal discussions, once the report had reached a final version, each member of the advisory council had the possibility of adding a dissenting opinion. This is common practice but, given that the report is a finely balanced compromise that has been reached through long consultations and difficult negotiations, I was in favor of not taking advantage of such a possibility. So I invited all members to make an extra effort to agree on the outcome. Some of us decided to opt for such a conciliatory approach. Compromises have the distinctive property of leaving each party a bit dissatisfied. Our report is not an exception. But I hope that those who will discuss it will use it not to take it apart, but to make further progress on an issue so vital for the future of the Internet.

We are the transitional generation. In the future, both people in front and behind a desk during a job interview, for example, will be digital natives. When everybody will be on the other side of the divide, embarrassing pictures on Facebook may just be normal and acceptable. An analogy may be drawn with prenuptial sex—something normal today, but still scandalous only a couple of generations ago.

How our culture and our notions of privacy and freedom of speech will change is very hard to guess but change they will. They are dynamic features of our social life and will evolve with it. I hope that they will change for the better, in favor of more relaxed and tolerant views of what, in the future, will be our personal information online. And I trust that more ideas, better technological solutions and new legal frameworks will provide for a reconciliation of privacy and freedom of expression—two necessary pillars of any liberal democracy.

# Periodical and Internet Sources Bibliography

*The following articles have been selected to supplement the diverse views presented in this chapter.*

Emerson T. Brooking and P. W. Singer, "War Goes Viral: How Social Media Is Being Weaponized Across the World," *Atlantic,* November 2016. https://www.theatlantic.com/magazine /archive/2016/11/war-goes-viral/501125.

Jeremy Gillula, et al., "Debate Simmers over Digital Privacy," Council on Foreign Relations, January 28, 2015. http://www.cfr.org /terrorism-and-technology/debate-simmers-over-digital-privacy /p36037.

Andy Greenberg, "How a 'Deviant' Philosopher Built Palantir, a CIA-Funded Data-Mining Juggernaut," *Forbes,* August 14, 2013. https://www.forbes.com/sites/andygreenberg/2013/08/14/agent -of-intelligence-how-a-deviant-philosopher-built-palantir-a-cia -funded-data-mining-juggernaut/#7bff14a57785.

Jamil N. Jaffer and Daniel J. Rosenthal, "Why Apple's Stand Against the F.B.I. Hurts Its Own Customers," *New York Times,* April 8, 2016. https://www.nytimes.com/2016/04/09/opinion/why-apples -stand-against-the-fbi-hurts-its-own-customers.html.

Newseum Institute, "Apple vs. FBI Resources." http://www .newseuminstitute.org/news/exchange/apple-vs-fbi-resources.

Nausicaa Renner, "A Loophole in the Right to Be Forgotten," *Columbia Journalism Review,* July 26, 2016. http://www.cjr.org /tow_center/loophole_google_right_forgotten.php.

Michael Sheetz, "The Rise of Tech-Savvy Global Terrorism Networks," CNBC, December 4, 2015. http://www.cnbc.com/2015/12/04 /the-everyday-technology-helping-terrorists-plot-evil.html.

Jeffrey Toobin, "The Solace of Oblivion," *New Yorker,* September 29, 2014. http://www.newyorker.com/magazine/2014/09/29/solace -oblivion.

**GLOBAL**VIEWPOINTS

# CHAPTER 3

# Tech Giants and Corporate Social Responsibility

# Tech Giants Are Uniquely Positioned to Give Back to Society

*Simon Morfit*

*In the following viewpoint, Simon Morfit argues that the traditional corporate social responsibility (CSR) model is a poor fit for today's tech giants. CSR refers to the strategies corporate entities employ to improve environmental, economic, and social conditions. For traditional manufacturing concerns, CSR usually means improved working conditions or a factory with a lighter environmental footprint. When it comes to tech giants, however, employees are often well-compensated (even pampered) and few operate factories. Morfit proposes several ways tech companies can harness their engineering prowess to create a new CSR paradigm. Morfit holds a PhD in sociology from the University of California, Berkeley.*

As you read, consider the following questions:

1. What two reasons does the author cite for why the CSR framework of traditional manufacturing won't work with the tech sector?
2. What is a "hackathon"?
3. What is Google's "Person Finder" application?

The success of the technology sector—the online platforms and services that have rapidly proliferated in recent years, distinct from material technology such as hardware and physical

"What Does Corporate Social Responsibility Mean for the Technology Sector?" by Simon Morfit, Stanford University, October 03, 2014. Reprinted by permission.

devices—is becoming increasingly conspicuous. The industry faces mounting calls to make greater societal contributions beyond those of profit. The technology field is uniquely positioned to give back to society in ways that distinguish it from other industries.

Concerns about the technology sector's social contract are particularly acute in California's San Francisco Bay Area, home to the majority of the country's technology companies and the hotbed of growing discontent toward the industry's success. Throughout the region, the technology field is blamed for gentrification and a cost of living that now ranks among the nation's highest. Resentment against the industry has bubbled over in such dramatic manifestations as the now well-known blockades of Google buses transporting San Francisco residents to their work in Mountain View, and union protestors surrounding Twitter's headquarters to decry tax breaks given to the company. At the heart of these debates lie concerns about how the technology industry interacts with the surrounding cities and communities in which it works. The sector's success contributes to divisions between the technology industry and all things non-tech. Protestors criticize the inequalities that accompany this separation and advocate for the industry to make greater returns to society.

Importantly, calls for the technology sector to give back do not exclusively come from those working in other, non-technology related, industries. Salesforce CEO Marc Benioff offers a prime example. He pioneered Salesforce's 1-1-1 community service model and championed the SF Gives campaign, an effort to get leading technology companies to donate $500,000 each to Tipping Point, a San Francisco foundation dedicated to poverty alleviation.

Benioff's contributions are unquestionably important—both in terms of generating greater resources for the social sector and of shifting the cultural norms of the technology industry to embrace the notion of giving back more readily. However, for a field that prides itself on innovation, the prevailing manner in which the technology sector is giving back looks a lot like every other industry: corporate philanthropy and volunteer campaigns.

This begs the question: Are there unique ways that the information technology sector can give back, and if so, what are they? The answer lies in invigorating how the sector pursues corporate responsibility (CSR) strategies.

CSR strategy has evolved considerably from where it was just a few years ago. It is now commonplace for major companies to have in-house CSR divisions and strategies that they can feature prominently in annual reports. However, this evolution has been uneven. Some sectors, especially those grounded in traditional manufacturing (such as the production of material goods), have made considerable advances in defining and implementing responsible business practices. Traditional manufacturing's means of production lends itself to the development of responsibility strategies. From T-shirts to coffee, CSR frameworks protect the wellbeing of labor and the environment. The production process outlines a roadmap around which companies can develop responsibility measures. Businesses attempting to strengthen their responsibility position can examine the human and environmental externalities that exist at each step in the sequence of creating a material good to arrive at responsibility strategies.

However, this degree of clarity does not exist for the technology sector. Analyzing the industry's production process does not illuminate responsibility strategies as it does for traditional manufacturing. On the human side, labor protections take a very different form than they do for other fields. The notion of a vulnerable line worker is replaced with that of a well-compensated programmer. Environmental concerns center on and are largely confined to reducing carbon emissions by increasing the computing efficiency of data equipment. What has become a conventional approach to developing responsibility strategies simply does not suit the technology sector very well, nor does it address the main criticisms the industry faces.

Technology professionals and their critics are wrestling with what it means to give back and what it looks like. Although we do not have full and clear answers to these questions, promising practices are emerging, and they deserve greater attention.

Hackathons—events that bring together computer programmers to intensively work on a new product or challenge for a concentrated amount of time—are a common technique to spur innovation in the technology field. Some are applying this approach to address social concerns. For instance, earlier this year, Cloudera, a leading developer of big-data solutions, hosted a hackathon to support AtrocityWatch, a nonprofit working to prevent crimes against humanity through crowd sourcing and data analysis.

The San Francisco Citizens Initiative for Technology and Innovation (sf.citi) offers another example. Sf.citi, a membership organization comprised of Bay Area technology companies, strives to foster partnerships between its members and government offices to tackle city problems through the power of technology. Thus far, sf.citi has supported pilot projects, consulting efforts, and software development to improve how city departments working on transportation and public safety collect and analyze data, thereby improving their operational efficiency.

Although criticized by protestors, larger, more established technology companies are also supporting social sector efforts. Google's Person Finder web application, for example, allows individuals to post and search for friends and relatives following emergencies (such as the Boston Marathon bombing). The application is configured to permit nonprofits and government agencies to contribute and receive data. Following the 2010 Haiti earthquake, Google shared mapping data with the United Nations and other relief agencies.

These examples represent what the technology sector excels at: capturing, analyzing, and sharing data. They also exemplify the greatest value-add that the technology industry can offer the social sector: data analytics. The ability of social sector organizations to obtain, handle, and act on information remains somewhat underdeveloped, especially in comparison to their for-profit

# The Lack of Diversity in Tech Is a Cultural Issue

A recent survey of the top 9 tech companies in Silicon Valley by *Fortune* reveals that on average, women comprise about one-third of the workforce. That gap expands the higher up you go in an organization, with the best company showing women holding 29% of leadership jobs. In general, companies made slightly better progress on ethnic diversity than they did on increasing their percentages of female employees, although not in leadership roles.

It has been a commonly held belief that the gender gap in tech is primarily a pipeline issue; that there are simply not enough girls studying math and science. Recently updated information indicates an equal number of high school girls and boys participating in STEM electives, and at Stanford and Berkeley, 50% of the introductory computer science students are women. That may be the case, but the U.S. Census Bureau reported last year that twice as many men as women with the same qualifications were working in STEM fields.

A *USA Today* study discloses that top universities graduate black and Hispanic computer science and computer engineering students at twice the rate that leading technology companies hire them. Although these companies state they don't have a qualified pool of applicants, the evidence does not support that claim.

If it's not a pipeline issue, why don't we see a greater representation of minorities and women in STEM industries?

The answer is we don't see more progress because the pipeline concern is not the primary reason for the discouraging statistics. There's a bigger issue. It's the culture. We can attempt to solve the problem by educating more women and minorities and challenging hiring practices which are all important initiatives, but the underlying issue that must be addressed to solve this problem is the hidden and often overt discrimination that prevails in the tech industry.

The reality is that gender and racial bias is so ubiquitous in the technology industry that it forces talented female and minority employees to leave. Companies can hire more minorities and women but without addressing this critical issue, they will not experience improvement in diversity.

*"The Lack of Diversity in Tech Is a Cultural Issue," by Bonnie Marcus, Forbes, August 12, 2015.*

counterparts. Rudimentary means of collecting, analyzing, and communicating information undermine the efficiency and impact of the social sector. A stronger information capacity can help social sector organizations understand the needs of beneficiaries and communities, target resources effectively, evaluate the impact of programs and services, and leverage big-data to anticipate and respond to challenges.

In short, we can use the technology sector's greatest asset to address a common weakness of social sector organizations. Strategies that make innovative contributions to how the social sector collects, interprets, and responds to data can also serve as vehicles for earning trust and building public support. These approaches hold enormous potential for the advancement of CSR; they also begin to answer important questions about how the technology sector can best give back to society.

# Tech Giants' Political Activism Reveals Opportunistic Altruism

*Kate Losse*

*In the following excerpted viewpoint, Kate Losse scrutinizes Facebook's lobbying efforts. In 2013, Facebook's CEO, Mark Zuckerberg, founded FWD, a lobbying coalition largely focused on immigration reform. But FWD's mission has an opportunistic air. "Like Facebook's other top-down 'revolutions,'" Losse writes, "[FWD] will primarily be advocating for the interest of its privileged, influential few." The author uses this example to explore the discord between global realities and Silicon Valley's idealism. Losse has written for the* New Yorker *and the* New York Times. *Her memoir,* The Boy Kings: A Journey Into the Heart of the Social Network, *chronicles her experience working at Facebook; she was the company's 51st employee and eventually served as Zuckerberg's speechwriter.*

As you read, consider the following questions:

1. How did FWD's first commercial rewrite Emma Lazarus's poem "The New Colossus"?
2. How do FWD's different ad campaigns target viewers on opposite ends of the ideological spectrum?
3. What action does the author consider "automatic activism"?

"Mr. Zuckerberg Goes to Washington," by Kate Losse, *Dissent Magazine*, 2013. Reprinted with permission of the University of Pennsylvania Press.

A s Silicon Valley companies have grown, with skyrocketing profits and public approbation, their executives have been startled recently to encounter an obstacle beyond their control: government regulation. Facebook now employs enough H1-B visa holders to trigger limits on its employment of high-tech immigrant workers. For a company that has built a global empire on "sharing," or moving user data through Facebook's system as freely as possible, the prospect of limits—whether on the distribution of data or human resources—is not welcome. Facebook's slogan, "move fast and break things," takes as a given that the company is firmly in the driver's seat, choosing its speed and what limits it will surpass, without its pace regulated by outside forces. Accustomed to relative technical sovereignty, Facebook and its cohort see the prospect of federal immigration restrictions not as a divergence of their interests with that of the public, but as an outdated threat from Washington, the imposition of old values on an ecosystem that has transcended them. "Lobbyists for Silicon Valley say those provisions are unworkable," wrote the *New York Times* in May regarding measures in the Senate immigration bill that prohibit tech companies from laying off American workers within three months of hiring guest workers.

So like any CEO reckoning with government regulation, Facebook's Mark Zuckerberg founded a political lobby, FWD.us. The lobby represents not only Facebook but a range of Silicon Valley startup founders and investors who share FWD's interest in advocating for the industry's autonomy. FWD marks tech's high-profile entry into politics. In working to protect its constituents' ability to, as FWD's slogan goes, "move the knowledge economy forward" rather than share power with others, FWD is much like any corporate lobby created to advocate and protect its founders' interests. But unlike traditional corporate lobbies, and in keeping with Facebook's tendency to represent its initiatives not as elite efforts but as "revolutionary movements," FWD is described by its founders not as representing a narrow set of corporate interests but as a new post- or non-partisan American coalition. "Our voice carries a lot of weight because we are broadly popular with Americans," the group claims in its prospectus, imagining that the popularity of its technical products is coterminous with the popularity of its leadership. For denizens of Silicon Valley, technical innovation is a sign of aptitude for all other types of innovation, and as a result FWD representatives speak with a general sense of authority; according to the *Times*, former Facebook executive and FWD backer Chamath Palihapitiya "argued that Fwd.us needs to be 'disruptive' in politics, as in commerce." On FWD's website, Zuckerberg pronounces current immigration policy "unfit for today's world."

Understanding the FWD vision for "today's world" is important because the lobby is directing millions of dollars at revising how Americans judge the merit of other people. A close reading of the arguments that FWD presents indicates as much about their ambitions for the American workforce as did Henry Ford's famous melting pot ceremony, wherein immigrant factory workers who had attended the Ford's assimilationist night school would jump into a "melting pot" in garb from their home country and emerge in American suits. The image still lingers in popular discourse, shaping how we see ourselves as a nation. Ford sought a homogenous, disciplined set of low-skill workers. What does Silicon Valley want?

[…]

In FWD's first advertisement, called "Emma," the lobby rewrites the classic Emma Lazarus poem, "The New Colossus," inscribed on the Statue of Liberty, which implores the world to "Give me your tired, your poor, / Your huddled masses yearning to breathe free, / The wretched refuse of your teeming shore, / Send these, the homeless, tempest-tost to me…." FWD converts these famous lines to: "Give me your tired, your poor / Your huddled masses yearning to breathe free / And give me the influencers and the dreamers / Talent that is searching for purpose / Those dedicated to the doing / Send all these, the boundless borne to me…." The altered verse recasts immigration as a talent search for "influencers" and "dreamers" in a world imagined as a field of visionary tech

## What Tech Giants Are Spending Millions Lobbying For

Tech companies already own Silicon Valley, but new lobbying disclosure documents reveal just how much weight they throw around Washington as well.

In the second quarter of 2015, Google spent a whopping $4.62 million on lobbying efforts. That's just slightly less than the $5.47 million they spent in the first quarter, but it still makes the search giant the third largest corporate lobbyist. Facebook increased its spend from $2.44 million to $2.69 million in the second quarter, while Amazon's budget grew from $1.91 million to $2.15 million. Meanwhile, Apple spent just $1.23 million of its huge mountain of cash.

But while the these sizable figures themselves are worthy of notice, it's equally important to consider just what policies these companies are lobbying for. While their policy concerns are not altogether surprising, they do tell a cohesive story about what the tech giants driving the industry consider to be its most pressing issues.

Immigration issues also topped the list as the companies lobbied the government to create more pathways for high-skilled foreign workers. It's a topic about which Facebook CEO Mark Zuckerberg has been particularly outspoken, going so far as to launch an advocacy group called Fwd.us back in 2013 with the explicit mission of fixing the immigration system.

The companies also prioritized taxation and trade policies. Facebook lobbied for the extension of the R&D tax credit. Amazon lobbyists, meanwhile, pursued the issue of the Remote Transactions Parity Act of 2015, an internet sales tax Amazon has endorsed that would require online stores to pay taxes in each state in which they sell goods.

Most of these issues are perennial topics for tech businesses in Washington. But the disclosure forms also reveal cottage interests of each company. Google, for instance, which has a substantial footprint in schools already thanks to its Chromebooks, pushed policymakers to promote the issue of connected education. Apple lobbied the Justice Department on issues related to government requests for data, which CEO Tim Cook has publicly opposed. And Amazon, determined to some day deliver packages by drone, lobbied the FAA and others on issues surrounding the regulation of unmanned aerial vehicles.

*"What Tech Giants Are Spending Millions Lobbying For," by Issie Lapowsky, Wired.com, July 23, 2015.*

industry candidates. The problem that FWD wants immigration to solve is not poverty or want or political persecution, but the problem of the technical person who is not yet fully exploited.

FWD's ad defines the "right" kind of immigrant. The rhetoric of the "influencer" is directly derived from social media, referring to the person who creates trends, the person who stands out from the mass rather than belonging to it. Influencers have "impact," in Facebook's oft-used recruiting language (the word appears four times on Facebook's Careers page); they have high scores on Klout, a website that ranks people's social impact based on the ongoing sum of their social media interactions—how they engage the masses with their brand. The rhetoric of the influencer is part of a breathless tech recruiting jargon where everyone is a singular, self-directed "entrepreneur" even while they are being recruited to work on big teams in large corporations. FWD's "influencer" thus becomes a new form of identity—the technical innovator who is always innovative regardless of what he or she is doing—that is privileged over others, not for insidious racial reasons but for deserving, meritocratic ones.

FWD has defined the "wrong" kind of immigrant, too. Part of the lobby's strategy has been to fund both liberal and conservative ads in support of comprehensive immigration reform. On the conservative side, the FWD-created group Americans for a Conservative Direction advocates, in an advertisement called "Strong," for FWD's plan to secure borders with drones, radar, fencing, and 20,000 new border agents, all while withholding green cards and benefits from immigrants in the process. The message, replete with ominous music and gunsight graphics, could not be more different from that in the Emma ad. Here, immigration policy needs to be reformed so that the wrong kind of immigrants—those who attempt to immigrate through the border rather than by applying for technical visas—are kept out.

FWD imagines the United States not as a country at all so much as a technical company. "Recruiting is the most important thing our company does. Immigration is recruiting for the country," reads a quote from Airbnb founder Brian Chesky posted on FWD founder Joe Green's Twitter feed. This logic echoes Zuckerberg's oft-repeated belief in "companies over countries," wherein "if you want to change the world, the best thing to do is start a company"; we can surmise that the best thing a country can do is to start functioning like a Silicon Valley company. In this, FWD reverses the power relationship that makes its founders' companies subject to inefficient, innovation-crushing government rule. It is the nation's government that needs to transform immigration into a process like company hiring, not companies that need to follow immigration law.

But just as companies cannot function on technical employees alone, nor can a country consist solely of "influencers." Meritocracy requires a group of the undeserving in order to promote the deserving, and the influencer requires that there be a mass of the influenced: a group who follows or participates rather than leads. Thus FWD's rhetoric of a nation of "influencers" is as paradoxical as Silicon Valley's recruiting rhetoric, in which companies are said to be composed fully of entrepreneurs: if everyone is leading, who or what is being led?

We can find one answer in the modern-day technology company, where technical workers are promoted as flagship employees while other types of employees often go underpaid and unacknowledged (contracting and hourly pay often distinguishes non-technical staff from the boldface entrepreneurial employees). That is, despite bombastic recruiting rhetoric, not everyone is imagined as an "influencer" at these companies, and those who aren't are rendered invisible. And because "influence" is defined from the top as a technical quality, rather than one that applies to other types of work like customer relations, content production, or administrative support, the marginalization of those who are "not technical" can be justified as the worker's failure to practice a valuable, influential skill. The privilege accorded to technical workers (and to their visa issues) is continuously reaffirmed by technical ideology while the working issues of others can go unrecognized.

[...]

What does politics look like in a nation dominated by influencers? That world is imagined in Facebook's 2012 ad, "The Things that Connect Us." The ad begins with an image of a floating chair and, in the course of explaining how chairs are like Facebook because they are where people sit and share, ends up arguing for the way that nations are like Facebook. The ad performs a transmutation of the country into a corporate entity by positing a contrast between the universe, which is "dark" and "makes us wonder if we are alone," and Facebook, which is a "great nation" that "makes us feel like we are not." Nationhood for Facebook users, of course, is not membership in a country but membership in a social network, and the video begins by depicting scenes of people sharing social moments with one another. It then builds to a climax by depicting various masses of people gathered together. But these crowds are gathered not for political but for social purposes, like weddings and athletic events, in which everyone celebrates in sync. In the final scene a massive crowd is assembled in the nation's capital, but the scene is entirely without conflict, more like a celebratory presidential inauguration than a political protest. The role of the mass, it appears, is to share, and when the mass acts it is to support, not challenge or dispute, its leadership.

The forms of action FWD proposes its supporters perform recapitulate this model of mass-choreographed political participation. FWD asks Facebook users to support FWD's immigration reforms by calling their senators through an application developed by FWD for Facebook. In this mode of nearly automatic activism we see that the frictionless sharing Facebook enables is at its most frictionless when it is working in support of Facebook's leadership. By virtue of their influential position, these leaders are able to program both their desired political content and the means by which the content is shared. The job of the user is to share the memes that they create—to sit in the symbolic chairs they have built for their users and connect socially.

The frictionlessness of sharing on Facebook is also what makes it attractive to people whose goal is to challenge Facebook's or other institutions' power, as, for example, the startup Upworthy intends to do. The company, founded by MoveOn.org founder Eli Pariser, creates political memes through social media. But as groups like Women, Action, and the Media (WAM!) have recently discovered when they attempted to lead protests against Facebook on Facebook (WAM! created the hashtag #fbrape and encouraged people to use it online to protest Facebook's lack of action to remove violent, misogynistic content), no amount of sharing on Facebook is enough to make Facebook's leadership cede its power to users and respond to their demands. WAM! has been understandably dismayed at Facebook's response to the #fbrape campaign, which has allowed violent content to remain on Facebook while allowing advertisers to remove their ads from reported pages. But demanding that the tool you use to circulate your message also submit to your message misunderstands the power dynamics of the platform. Just as in another Facebook ad, "Home," where a disruptive employee resists Zuckerberg's instructions by using Facebook, all that matters to the technology's leadership is that people use it. Insofar as people continue to use it, even in protest and replete with angry hashtags, the tool's dominance remains unthreatened.

As was the case in the #fbrape protest, technical platforms seeking massive scale frequently opt for system-wide efficiency over individual users' demands. In the case of FWD's advocacy for the H1-B visa expansion, the concerns of individual H1-B visa applicants happily align with the system's scalability—more visas are good for both the visa applicant and the company seeking to hire them. This coincidence of FWD's interests and H1-B visa applicants' interests, however, is not evidence that FWD is concerned with the specific immigrant issues represented by groups like the National Guestworker Alliance, just as tech's recent interest in leading in other areas like feminism and school reform does not mean that its leadership is concerned with issues that everyday women or teachers face. The target of FWD's reforms is efficient corporate recruiting, not improving the lives of all immigrants. This is why, once these innovator-specific reforms have passed, we should not be surprised if broader advocacy for immigration and worker issues fails to follow.

In his *Washington Post* op-ed announcing FWD, Zuckerberg wrote, "This can change everything. In a knowledge economy, the most important resources are the talented people we educate and attract to our country." FWD, like all of Facebook's initiatives that conflate the leadership of the powerful with transformation for all, is pushing the interests of the tech industry forward in the name of all immigrant workers. But like Facebook's other top-down "revolutions," it will primarily be advocating for the interests of its privileged, influential few.

# Twitter's Impact on the 2016 Presidential Election Is Unmistakable

*Shontavia Johnson*

*In the following viewpoint, Shontavia Johnson argues that, based on the 2016 US presidential election, Twitter will transform the way presidential campaigns are managed in the future. Disruptive technologies, such as radio and television, have altered elections throughout US history. Today, data shows that social media can have a profound effect on voters' opinions of candidates. Trump's management of his own Twitter account allowed him to connect with voters in a way that his opponent, Hillary Clinton, whose account was managed by staff, did not. Further, his incendiary tweets often were so outrageous that they were covered by mass media outlets, gaining him free publicity. What seemed shocking and "unpresidential" may be the new normal. Johnson is professor of intellectual property law at Drake University.*

"Donald Trump Tweeted Himself into the White House," by Shontavia Johnson, The Conversation, November 10, 2016. https://theconversation.com/donald-trump-tweeted-himself-into-the-white-house-68561. Licensed under CC BY-ND 4.0 International.

As you read, consider the following questions:

1. How many active Twitter users were there in the three quarters of 2016, leading up to the presidential election?
2. What emotion did Trump play to when trying to spread his message?
3. What technology did John F. Kennedy credit for helping him win the election?

Donald Trump's presidential election victory has been described as stunning, shocking and having elicited a "primal scream" from the media. The president-elect resonated enough with more than 59 million Americans that they pulled the lever for him in the voting booth and propelled him to a win.

Trump connected with his supporters both in person and on social media, particularly via Twitter. He was back tweeting mere hours after delivering his victory speech.

> Such a beautiful and important evening! The forgotten man and woman will never be forgotten again. We will all come together as never before

Trump's affinity for Twitter is well-documented. One political operative characterized the candidate's presence on the social networking site as "a continuous Trump rally that happens on Twitter at all hours." His perceived dexterity led some to declare him the best on social media and winner of the social media war.

But how much influence did Twitter have during the 2016 presidential election? As a law professor who researches the internet's impact on the tangible world, I believe the answer to this question could, in some ways, transform the way political candidates manage their campaigns for years to come.

## Politics in the Palm of Your Hand

With more than 300 million active users in the first three-quarters of 2016, Twitter allows people to interact with droves of friends and followers in 140 characters or less. While Americans tend to avoid discussions about politics offline, social media environments like Twitter make it nearly impossible to avoid political interactions on the internet. Though research shows that few Clinton or Trump supporters have close friends in the opposing camp, social media extends these connections significantly. With Twitter in particular, users are statistically more likely to follow people they do not know personally than with Facebook, where users often connect to those with whom they have some personal connection.

This is particularly powerful when you consider the impact social media has on political opinions. Long hours of exposure to political discourse can enhance participation in politics, and communication with others galvanizes political activity around common concerns. One in five people report changing their views on a political or social issue because of something they read on social media, and nearly the same amount say they changed their views about a specific candidate based on what they read there.

## Trump's Uncensored Tweets Persuaded

Trump was remarkably effective at harnessing this type of social media power to influence opinions. His campaign successfully crowdsourced a message of anger and fear by leveraging the knowledge, contacts and skills of his followers to disseminate his tweets widely. For example, Trump would receive nearly double the number of Twitter mentions as Hillary Clinton each day, even though (or maybe because) his messages were much more negative. He also boasted about 40 percent more Twitter followers than his democratic rival.

Trump developed a rapport with his followers by maintaining his own Twitter account throughout much of his campaign. Clinton primarily used a media team—and it showed. Experts have pointed out that because Trump's tweets largely sounded like they came directly from him—seeming off-the-cuff and unvetted by media pros—they were quite persuasive for his supporters.

This type of relationship development proved to be critical, as fans and followers joined Trump's movement and developed into large voting blocs. Scott Adams, who created the "Dilbert" comic strip, spent much of the election season writing about Trump as a master of persuasion, particularly through his strong use of fear.

Quantitatively, Trump's apparently unfiltered posts reiterating this messaging regularly resulted in much more Twitter engagement for him than Clinton. Trump's followers would replicate and share his message in droves. Some described having an "emotional connection" to him and would spend hours pushing his message to their own networks, even though they were not officially affiliated with the Trump campaign.

In addition, Trump's posts created a feedback loop, whereby posts on social media made it to television news—getting for free what would have cost the equivalent of US$3 billion in media coverage and advertising costs. He ultimately spent less money per vote and per delegate than anyone running for president this year, but obtained the highest level of visibility.

This is not to suggest that Clinton didn't have her own successes. Responding to an insult from Trump, she earned the most retweeted tweet of the campaign season when she suggested that Trump delete his Twitter account.

But Trump monopolized Twitter and the news cycle and ultimately obtained the most electoral votes.

## Harnessing the Tech of the Day

Historians have noted that disruptive technologies have the power to transform political elections. Franklin D. Roosevelt used the new medium of radio to deliver his fireside chats because his opponents controlled many of the newspapers in the 1930s and he wanted to avoid newspaper bias. John F. Kennedy, four days after narrowly defeating Richard Nixon, stated that "it was the TV more than anything else that turned the tide." Television, the new medium of the day, had exploded in popularity during the decade preceding the 1960 election. It seems that Trump took several pages out of history to help pull off one of the biggest upsets in modern election history.

I imagine researchers will study Trump's campaign tactics for years to come. In fact, analyses of Twitter's impact on the 2016 presidential election have already begun. The New York Times even recently cataloged all of the "people, places, and things" Trump insulted on Twitter. Trump's unconventional methods, originally ridiculed by traditional pundits as ineffective and sounding like a "rushed, high school term paper," thrived on Twitter's quick and unfiltered universe. His campaign could test acerbic messages in near real-time with his followers and determine whether to continue them on the campaign trail.

Traditional politicians looking to remain in office may discover that Trump's unconventional rise has created a new normal for campaign strategies. Unsurprisingly, Twitter users whose posts get a lot of engagement through likes, retweets and replies post more frequently than users who do not. And research also shows that emotions on Twitter are contagious—both negative and positive tweets generate more of the same on the platform (with positive tweets being more contagious). As emotion played a role in this year's political campaign, unlocking the secrets to wide and permanent dissemination will bode well for political candidates who harness the power of Twitter and other social media forms… at least until the next innovation comes along.

# Curating Our Online Content Creates Long-term Problems

*Jon Martindale*

*In the following viewpoint, Jon Martindale examines the role filter bubbles play in today's political landscape. Martindale also plumbs the preponderance of fake news and misinformation's historical precedents (it concerned Plato and John Adams). All the while, he wonders at the sometimes perilous commingling of emotion and reporting. Although we pay a hefty price for a personalized internet experience, all is not lost. There are very real things users can do to break free of online filter bubbles. Martindale is a freelance journalist based in the United Kingdom.*

As you read, consider the following questions:

1. What is a "filter bubble"?
2. According to Mark Zuckerberg, what percentage of Facebook news does fake new account for?
3. How does Eli Pariser think artificial intelligence can help solve the problem of filter bubbles and fake news?

It's been half a decade since the co-founder of Avaaz, Eli Pariser, first coined the phrase "filter bubble," but his prophetic TED Talk—and his concerns and warnings—are even more applicable now than they were then. In an era of fake news, curated content, personalized experiences, and deep ideological divisions, it's time we all take responsibility for bursting our own filter bubbles.

When I search for something on Google, the results I see are quite different from yours, based on our individual search histories and whatever other data Google has collected over the years. We see this all the time on our Facebook timelines, as the social network uses its vats of data to offer us what it thinks we want to see and hear. This is your bubble.

Numerous companies have been striving toward bubbles for years. Facebook founder and CEO Mark Zuckerberg is believed to have once told colleagues that "a squirrel dying in your front yard may be more relevant to your interests right now than people dying in Africa." The entirety of Facebook is geared toward making sure you know everything there is to know about that squirrel.

Although contentious, it's arguable that Zuckerberg is at least partly right. People couldn't function in their day-to-day lives if they spent every second worrying about the problems of the world. But curating our news to give us what we want to see, rather than what we perhaps need to see, has real, long-term problems.

## The Dangers of Filter Bubbles

Filter bubbles may not seem too threatening a prospect, but they can lead to two distinct but connected issues. The first is that when you only see things you agree with, it can lead to a snowballing confirmation bias that builds up steadily over time.

A wider problem is that with such difference sources of information between people, it can lead to the generation of a real disconnect, as they become unable to understand how anyone could think differently from themselves.

A look at any of the left- or right-leaning mainstream TV stations during the buildup to the recent election would have left you in no doubt over which candidate they backed. The same can be said of newspapers and other media. In fact, this is true of many published endorsements.

But we're all aware of that bias. It's easy to simply switch off or switch over to another station, to see the other side of the coin.

Online, the bias is more covert. Google searches, social network feeds, and even some news publications all curate what they show you. Worse, it's all behind the scenes. They don't overtly take a stance, they invisibly paint the digital landscape with things that are likely to align with your point of view.

If a person's Facebook feed is full of pro-Hillary and anti-Trump stories and posts, you may wonder how on Earth anyone could vote for the man. If your feed is the complete opposite, highlighting only the negatives of Hillary and championing Trump and his benefits, you may have the exact opposite opinion.

Like Wittgenstein's Lion, if our frames of reference from news and social feeds are so different from one another, could we ever hope to understand each other's position?

## Fake News, a Historic Problem, Persists Today

This becomes even more of a problem when you factor in faux news. This latest election was one of the most contentious in history, with low-approval candidates on both sides and salacious headlines thrown out by every source imaginable. With so much mud being slung, it was hard to keep track of what was going on, and that was doubly so online, where fake news was abundant.

This is something that Facebook CEO Mark Zuckerberg has tried to play down, claiming that it only accounted for 1 percent of the overall Facebook news. Considering Facebook has near 2 billion users, though, that's potentially a lot of faux stories parroted as the truth. It's proved enough of an issue that studies suggest many people have difficulty telling fake news from real news, and in the weeks since the election, both Google and Facebook have made pledges to deal with the problem.

Also consider that 61 percent of millennials use Facebook as their main source of news, and you can see how this issue could be set to worsen if it's not stoppered soon. But this isn't the first time the youth has been tricked by the right sort of lies.

Fake news, fake knowledge, and fake wisdom are something that humans have had difficulty with in perpetuity. Sophistry was once a practice of teaching rhetoric and public speaking in ancient Greece, but is thought to have been co-opted by charlatans who used the power of rhetoric and philosophy to not only make money from their paying students, but to popularize ridiculous arguments.

Plato described such a person in one of his later dialogues, and attempted to draw a comparison between them and their brand of implied wisdom, versus a true philosopher or statesman. In it, he concludes that sophistry is the near indistinguishable imitation of a true art, much as fake news today imitates the art form of journalistic investigation and reporting.

The second president of the United States, John Adams, knew its dangers too. In response to a letter from a friend in 1819 inquiring about the definition of certain words like "liberty and "republic," he praised the search for such clarity, highlighting the importance of being acutely aware of the meaning behind words and phrases.

"Abuse of words has been the great instrument of sophistry and chicanery, of party, faction, and division of society," he said, before citing his own tiredness at the pursuit of such clarification.

In much the same way that sophists and fraudsters of the past could use the techniques of their peers to make money, raise their own stature, and in some ways subvert the functioning society, fake news sites and authors use the styles and techniques of online journalism to create content that seems plausible. When combined with a salacious headline, and the ability to easily share that content online before checking its authenticity, you have a recipe for the proliferation of phony stories that can have a real cultural impact.

While Zuckerberg may not think fake news and memes made a difference to the election, Facebook employee and Oculus VR founder Palmer Luckey certainly did. He was outed earlier this year for investing more than $100,000 in a company that helped promote Donald Trump online through the proliferation of memes and inflammatory attack advertisements. He wouldn't have put in the effort if he thought it worthless.

## Stories Drive Emotions

Buzzfeed's analysis of the popular shared stories on Facebook shows that while fake news underperformed compared to its real counterparts in early 2016, by the time the Election Day rolled around at the start of November, it had a 1.5 million engagement lead over true stories.

That same analysis piece highlighted some of the biggest fake election stories, and all of them contained classic click-baiting tactics. They used scandalous wording, capitalization, and sensationalist claims to draw in the clickers, sharers, and commenters.

That's because these sorts of words help to draw an emotional reaction from us. Marketing firm Co-Schedule discovered this back in 2014, but it's likely something that many people would agree with even without the hard numbers. We've all been tempted by clickbait headlines before, and they're usually ones that appeal to fear, anger, arousal, or some other part of us that isn't related to critical thinking and political analysis. Everyone's slinging mud from within their own filter bubbles, secure in the knowledge that they are right, and that everyone who thinks differently is an idiot.

## Bursting What You Cannot See

And therein lies the difficulty. The only way to really understand why someone may hold a different viewpoint is through empathy. But how can you empathize when you don't have control over how the world appears to you, and your filter serves as a buffer to stories that might help you connect with the other side?

Reaching out to us from the past, Pariser has some thoughts for those of us now living through his warning of the future. Even if Facebook may be stripping all humanity from its news curation, there are still human minds and fingertips behind the algorithms that feed us content. He called on those programmers to instill a sense of journalistic integrity in the AI behind the scenes.

"We need the gatekeepers [of information] to encode [journalistic] responsibility into the code that they're writing. [...] We need to make sure that these algorithms have encoded in them a sense of the public life, a sense of civic responsibility. They need to be transparent enough that we can see what the rules are and [...] we need [to be] given some control."

That sort of suggestion seems particularly pertinent, since it was only at the end of August that Facebook laid off its entire editorial team, relying instead on automated algorithms to curate content. They didn't do a great job, though, as weeks later they were found to have let a bevy of faux content through the screening process.

While it may seem like a tall order for megacorporations to push for such an open platform, so much of a stink has been raised about fake news in the wake of the election that it does seem like Facebook and Google at least will be doing something to target that problematic aspect of social networking. They can do more, though, and it could start with helping to raise awareness of the differences in the content we're shown.

Certainly there are times we don't need content catered to us. If you are researching a topic to write on, you want the raw data, not Google's beautified version of it. When it comes to news, offering some manual control over the curation wouldn't go amiss. either.

How about a button that lets us see the complete opposite to what our data-driven, personalized feeds show? I'd certainly click that now and again.

But that puts the onus on other people to make the change for us, and it's important to remember that the reason these services feed us content that's relatively narrow is because of our own searches and clicks. If we all made a point to read outside of our comfort zone, to go in with a clear mind and demand content outside of our own bubble, we would get it and the algorithms would gradually respond.

That has the double benefit of giving us an immediate access to new information, but also teaches our digital curators to be a little more open-minded themselves.

And perhaps us too. At least enough to listen without shouting down and demanding a safe space for our own thoughts. Whether you believe that the opposing viewpoint is misguided, wrong, or disgusting, the best way to combat it is with reasonable debate. No terrible idea can survive the harsh light of day and intelligent opposition.

For his side of things, Pariser continues to highlight the problems filter bubbles pose, but has taken it upon himself to bring together people to help fight fake news and other online nonsense. If you'd like to help him out, you can contribute yourself.

It seems increasingly clear, though, that as much as there are many large institutions that need to make changes to help strive for truth online, the best step we can all take is to burst our own bubbles to see what's beyond. It just might make thing a little clearer in a time where it's increasingly hard to keep on top of what's what.

# Innovation Should Not Sacrifice Privacy and Free Speech

*United Nations Educational, Scientific and Cultural Organization*

*The following viewpoint is excerpted from a 2015 study conducted by the United Nations Educational, Scientific and Cultural Organization (UNESCO). The organization worked with UN member states and other stakeholders to analyze four keystones of internet universality: rights, openness, accessibility, and user-centric perspectives. The study explores the ways in which the internet "reconfigure[s] access to information and knowledge, and also reshape[s] freedom of expression, privacy, and ethical norms and behaviour." The selections here focus on privacy and anonymity; regulation of content, journalism, and free speech; and big data.*

As you read, consider the following questions:

1. Why is suppressing reporting in an effort to prevent copycats not a good idea?
2. How might the definition of "journalist" be expanded?
3. What is "big data" and what ethical dilemmas does it pose?

"Keystones to Foster Inclusive Knowledge Societies," The United Nations Educational, Scientific and Cultural Organization. March 4, 2015. http://www.unesco.org/new/fileadmin/MULTIMEDIA/HQ/CI/CI/pdf/Events/internet_draft_study_simple_version.pdf. Licensed under CC BY-SA 3.0 IGO.

## Challenges for the Digital Age—What Are the Ends that Technology Should Serve?

The global diffusion of the Internet is progressing, but at the same time what we know as the Internet is continually changing. Innovation continues apace in many areas, from mobile applications and payment systems to social media and ICT. This progress may seem like an unalloyed blessing, evident in the degree that the Internet has reached more people in more powerful ways than ever thought possible. It has also become a major resource for economic development. Fostering continued Internet innovation is an important goal, but the issues are broader than simply supporting technological innovation and diffusion (Mansell and Tremblay 2013).

As the Internet and related digital media have evolved, they have come to serve many diverse purposes for many different actors, from household entertainment to government surveillance. It is important, therefore, to consider the ends that this technology should serve, and what objectives and actions could be developed to encourage progress in these directions. In this respect, trends in technology, policy and patterns of Internet use raise important questions about its current and future social, cultural and economic uses and implications. For example, technical innovations are altering traditional business models, such as in the provision of news, and the structure of organisations, where traditional hierarchical reporting relationships have been challenged by many-to-one and many-to-many networks of communication that span organisational boundaries. As digital media have been a force behind the convergence of formerly more distinct technologies of the post, telephone, and mass media, so policy and regulation have often failed to keep up. This has left potentially inappropriate regulations in place and failed to integrate new solutions such as Media and Information Literacy. Likewise, technical change is being accompanied by changes in the habits of individuals: for instance, how households watch television, or how many households no longer perceive the need for a fixed-line telephone, once viewed as the gold standard of modern communication infrastructures, or even in how scientists collaborate.

These changes are simple illustrations of a wider array of worldwide social and technical trends that are likely to have unanticipated and potentially negative as well as positive consequences for human rights, such as press freedom, plus access, and the ethical use of communication technologies—unless they are well understood, better anticipated and appropriately addressed through policy and practice (UNESCO 2014d). The IoT, for example, could usher in major benefits, such as remote monitoring of patients. But it might also unintentionally undermine the privacy of individuals, unless this potential is recognized and avoided in the design and regulation of this innovative area of activity.

A worldwide ecology of policies and regulations is shaping the interrelated local and global outcomes of the Internet on access to information and knowledge, freedom of expression, privacy and ethics (Dutton et al. 2011; Mendel et al. 2012; MacKinnon et al. 2015; UNESCO 2013b). And such policy choices are being considered by a multiplicity of actors at all levels—from the local to national, regional and global, including governments, international organizations, civil society and non-governmental organizations (NGOs), technical communities, the private sector of business and industry, academia, individual users, and media organizations, such as the press, that rely increasingly on the Internet. All are concerned that the policies and practices governing the Internet could undermine principles and purposes they view as fundamental, whether those values are centred on freedom of expression, the privacy of personal information, or other ethical principles, and whether the implications are perceived to be immediate or long term.

[…]

> # Facebook to Roll Out Fake News Tools in Germany
>
> The world's largest social network said it would enable German users to flag potentially false stories.
>
> The stories will then be passed to third-party fact-checkers and if found to be unreliable, will be marked in users' news feeds as "disputed."
>
> Facebook has been widely criticised after some users complained that fake news had influenced the US presidential election.
>
> German government officials have expressed concern that misinformation on the internet could influence the country's parliamentary election this year.
>
> Under the new measures, users in Germany will be able to select "It's a fake news story" as an option when reporting another user's post.
>
> They can then mark the post as fake news, let the other user know they think it is fake, or block that user.
>
> Facebook will send potentially fake stories to Correctiv, a German non-profit body of investigative journalists, to check the facts.
>
> If they find a story to be false, it will be marked on Facebook as "disputed" and will appear lower in users' news feeds.
>
> The fact-checkers must sign up to a code of principles to take part. There are currently 43 signatories, including news organisations in several different countries.
>
> As in the US, Facebook Germany said it was looking into penalising websites, which tried to mimic major publishers or misled readers into thinking they were a well-known news source.
>
> *"Facebook to Roll Out Fake News Tools in Germany," BBC News, January 15, 2017.*

# Consultations on Promoting Freedom of Expression

### Blocking, Filtering and Content Regulation

Blocking and filtering of content was a very common area of concern, as these measures restrict in a direct way citizens' rights to express themselves freely, as well as impacting adversely on their right to access online content. In many cases, users might not even realize that content has been filtered or blocked. At the same time, there was some recognition that alongside censorship as a violation of free expression, there was also legitimate reason in some contexts to block certain content, such as material that incites violence. This raises the question of how to draw the line in specific cases about what to block, for how long, in what proportion, and with what transparency and redress mechanism. Historically, this judgement might have been relatively easier to apply. For instance, a common limitation on free speech is often cited as "shouting fire in a crowded theatre."[1] Today, there are legitimate fears that a video posted in one jurisdiction could incite violence in another. However, blame may be more appropriately attributed in some contexts to the actors, rather than the content, where the former exploit the content to instigate violence. Accordingly, content restrictions may be difficult to justify prior to any action, and actions in turn may be difficult to predict. Another consideration is that while reporting of some events, such as a suicide or a terrorist strike, could lead others to copycat actions, the importance of reporting accurate and trusted news may override the potential for such harms.

For such reasons, numerous respondents to the consultation identified content restriction by governments as a major threat to freedom of expression—on the basis that it can come to serve as, or morph into, censorship of legitimate speech. Alternatives were suggested as means to mitigate the presence and impact of illegitimate speech.

One of these was voluntary self-restriction on the part of users as a means for reducing the dangers of government censorship. However, self-restriction was identified as an area of concern as well, particularly if users increasingly believe their views are being followed by public authorities. That is, users, ISPs and other actors might over-restrict, thereby self-censoring online because they feel that their views might be sanctioned by government, or used to pro le them as in support or opposition to particular ideas or policies. Such anticipatory self-censorship can violate free expression even more than that imposed by governments directly censoring the

Internet. The matter of self-censorship, however, was seen as distinct from encouraging self-restriction as a matter of ethical choice, freely made, including through systems of voluntary and independent self-regulation aligned to international standards on free expression.

Respondents also raised the criminalization of online expression, including the criminal prosecution of online commentators, such as for violating law or policy that was developed to apply to broadcasters in an earlier media era. For example, if one user is arrested or prosecuted for posting an offensive remark, for instance on a news site, blog, or Twitter conversation, this could have a chilling effect on other users. The regulation applied is often based on law or policy designed to restrict broadcasting, given its reach and potential impact, whereas a tweet, for instance, is most likely to be read by very few, if any individuals, unless news coverage of the tweet brings it to the attention of a wider audience, such as when someone takes action against an offensive tweet. As more and more individuals are being prosecuted, concern was raised that more people will naturally worry about expressing themselves freely in such circumstances. Far from feeling that they are part of a global public commons, they will feel as if they are taking an unpredictable risk by exposing their views online.

Another issue raised by respondents was the danger of intermediary liability—making social media platforms or publishers, for example, responsible for an alleged case of hate speech. This measure, treating these actors as traditional analogue media, can have a chilling effect, and make them vulnerable to overcompensating and overly limiting expression, even when it does not violate international standards. This situation can escalate formal or informal takedown requests—and may lead intermediaries to take an overly aggressive proactive role in filtering content, that would also often not be visible or subject to transparency or accountability. If this role of intermediaries were to prevail, it would make ISPs and other intermediaries more like printed newspapers, in that they would become increasingly responsible for the editing of content; they might therefore be subject to lawsuits and other actions over libel, which would have further chilling effects on a free, trusted global Internet. For this reason, some respondents suggested that policies requiring platforms to self-regulate and police their own content could have a negative effect on freedom of expression. Others proposed that such systems could provide a first port of call for individuals to seek legitimate restrictions on content, with independent courts as a back up to decide whether contested decisions amounted to censorship or not.

As seen in analysing these issues, the problem of content regulation is a difficult one in general, because it entails considerations of interpreting international standards of legitimate processes, necessity and due purpose as regards any limitation of the right to free expression. It can be exercised by multiple actors, particularly intermediaries and governments, for example, but it can also be addressed by individual users, such as by identifying instances of censorship and exposing these cases to the court of public opinion. In such ways, the Internet has the potential for enabling individual Internet users to hold institutions and other users more accountable for their actions online, creating what has been called a "Fifth Estate," analogous to the Fourth Estate of the press, but potentially even more powerful (Dutton 2009). Nevertheless, a Fifth Estate requires a relatively free and open Internet to be sustainable and influential.

### User Targeting and Profiling
Also of concern amongst respondents was the ability of some actors, such as governments or commercial enterprises, to target individual users, given that they will know much about their interests through their search or other online activities. Even individual users of social media platforms can advertise to others who are interested in particular topics. Is this an exercise of free speech or a violation of privacy? A related issue raised is that of

the so-called "filter bubble" (Pariser 2011): the idea that different Internet users will see different versions of the Internet, based on their previous search preferences. User targeting can happen at the level of the government, private companies (such as search or social media providers), or even at the infrastructural level.

## Anonymity

The anonymity of users was seen as important to free expression, but also as under threat. This is important because anonymity is seen as a cornerstone of privacy; many respondents considered anonymity a prerequisite for the expression of unpopular or critical speech, although anonymity is a more protected right in some countries than in others. At the same time, anonymity is sometimes viewed as contributing to harmful speech that goes beyond international standards defining the legitimate exercise of the right to free expression, such as hate speech. Despite this perception, academic research has not established that the identification of speakers would be a cure to insensitive or hurtful remarks, since these are often fostered by a larger set of circumstances, such as a failure of users sitting at a computer to fully realise that they are communicating with a real person.

Anonymity may also impact on public debate online. In some countries, participants would refrain from participating (for instance on the issue of gay rights) for fear of identification and persecution. On the other hand, there is also the case of anonymous paid commentators who pose as self-selected users to kill debate, such as by scaring participants away by being discourteous or profane and thereby having a chilling effect on the expression of minority or unpopular views. At the same time, some government agencies have assigned personnel to follow and respond to online forums as a means to "join the conversation" and decrease the likelihood of misinformation by providing corrections or alternative sources of information and this can be positive if they identify themselves, such as in some cases of online diplomacy

(Khatib et al. 2012). Anonymity in cyberattacks, including fake domain attacks impersonating civil society, were of concern in terms of being serious violations of free expression.

[...]

## Network Neutrality

The major advocates of network neutrality wish to use government regulation to keep the Internet open and avoid the creation of so-called "fast lanes" for some Internet service providers, such as a film service that can afford to pay for faster access to a household, since a new rival company might not be able to compete with such a fast service. They would see this as potentially discriminatory and anti- competitive, with the removal of an "even-playing-field" impacting on those seeking to express content online. The critics of this policy believe market forces should be permitted to determine the wisdom of such fast lanes, and that net neutrality policy would usher in government regulation that would stifle innovation, such as by introducing government-imposed pricing of services. Advocates argue that whether governments begin to regulate Internet services for neutrality, does not necessarily mean they will seek to regulate prices or stifle innovation.

[...]

## Regulation and Freedom of Expression

Numerous respondents identified obstacles in maintaining and promoting the right to freedom of expression via regulation and regulatory frameworks. Some respondents saw the Internet as inherently unregulated, due to its globalized and borderless nature, and identified a difficulty in establishing effective state-based regulation in a world where content can be hosted and accessed from entirely different countries.

Some argued, therefore, that legislation alone could not protect freedom of expression; several others acknowledged that striking the correct regulatory balance would be a difficult challenge, as over- or inappropriate regulation could have negative consequences, not only for freedom of expression but for the value of the

Internet in general. In fact, a number of respondents highlighted excessive, restrictive regulation as problematic. They argued that governments should not restrict freedoms, but should rather ensure that fundamental human rights—including communication-related rights—are protected. Other respondents, by contrast, were concerned that deregulation would be a detriment to the public interest. One respondent proposed exploring experimental regulatory mechanisms as a means of developing a more evidence-based approach, but how this would be done was unclear.

Respondents felt that national laws are frequently in need of alignment with global rules, standards, and norms regarding freedom of expression rights. Some called for legislation protecting journalists, including expansion of the definition of "journalist" to include social media producers and human rights advocates, for example. Updating regulation that protects the confidentiality of journalists' sources to include digital aspects, was underlined as being central to press freedom in research specially commissioned from the World Association of Newspapers (WAN-IFRA) as a contribution towards this study.[2]

A number of respondents felt that Internet-specific laws to protect freedom of expression were justified, since the Internet is so very different from any of the traditional media that came before it. One justification was that the Internet's specific affordances, technical characteristics, and status as a network for the interchange of information and knowledge make existing legislation either outdated or disproportionately restrictive. Some also felt freedom of expression is particularly threatened on the Internet, and that authorities or others rely on the lack of Internet-specific legal protections to more easily prevent speech online. Others felt that there are specific needs to legally protect user privacy, prevent censorship of user content, or to guarantee anonymity, for instance, that are not covered by traditional media regulations.

Respondents also presented arguments against Internet-specific legislation. One concern was that good rules, norms, and laws already exist, but that either national adoption or effective enforcement is not up to standard. Some expressed concern that new legislation could introduce loopholes or avenues of exploitation. Others disagreed that the Internet is fundamentally different from existing media, and felt that freedom of expression rights can be established regardless of the medium. They felt that the differences between the offline and online worlds were not significant enough to require Internet-specific legislation. Still others felt that a focus on protecting human dignity was more important than protecting freedom of expression rights, or that freedom of expression should be strengthened everywhere, without specific reference to Internet-related problems.

Finally, some respondents were ambivalent or relativistic on the issue, arguing, for instance, that citizens in different polities should make their own democratic decisions as to the need for legislation. These arguments tended to suggest that different limits or boundaries on the right to freedom of expression might exist for different people, cultures, or even online platforms, albeit without transgressing the parameters of the broader international standards on this matter (transparency, legitimate purpose, necessity, proportionality, and so on). Some also argued for self-regulation (discussed above) as an alternative to government legislation, or for a general policy of government neutrality regarding the Internet. Self-regulation was again mentioned positively by some respondents, especially in areas such as journalistic ethics.

Respondents who argued in favour of regulation saw a need for effective, clear, legislation focused on human rights. Specifically, they argued that freedom of expression and privacy rights are fundamental human rights, and should be guaranteed as such in national constitutions. One complaint was also that regulation is often not 'user-friendly', either due to complex or onerous laws—such as those that have led to the arrest of social media users, for example, for posting a tweet deemed inappropriate by the authorities. And, as mentioned above, respondents identified the need, once regulatory frameworks are established, for consistent application of laws. Special concern was raised over governments violating their own rules, and also over a lack of knowledge by legislators, and by members of the judiciary. Respondents called for the implementation of existing standards, the need for effective compliance systems, and more guidance on how to comply with those standards. They called for the involvement of a wide variety of actors, especially civil society organizations, during the legislative drafting process, and felt that once established, regulatory bodies should be independent from government and private influence alike.

### Regulatory Challenges: Journalism

Journalistic practice is of special concern to freedom of expression. Two of the questionnaire items focussed on questions related to journalism. First, are journalists adequately protected by existing legislation in regard to their digital activities? And, second, what scope is there for journalistic self-regulation?

Though acknowledging regulatory variation between countries, some respondents felt that protections for journalists were inadequate, with many feeling that journalists were "barely" covered. Of prime concern by respondents was that protections, where they exist, are often limited to "traditional" journalists—those working in media such as print or broadcast. In an era of increasingly Internet-based journalism, this was seen as inadequate. Respondents motivated that these rights should exist regardless of medium. Some suggested a reframing of journalism as an activity (which any citizen can perform), rather than necessarily a profession.

There are some special challenges facing Internet journalism. In some countries, news sites must be authorized by the government, or certain material is prevented from being published (or in some cases, accessed). A second challenge is the rise in "citizen journalism," where citizens not trained as journalists are using new media, such as social media, to publish news. Though this can lead to positive competition with professional journalism, including ethical lapses in this sector, but also raising issues of ethics in social media production. Third, the interface with digital can mean that journalists are more easily targeted by elements interested in their sources or seeking to eliminate their output, or even to attack the journalists themselves. Security practices in regard to the Internet have threatened journalistic freedom in a number of cases.

In relation to these complexities, respondents identified several important areas of concern. Education of journalists was seen as critical. Such education could include ethical training, and the establishment of professional guidelines and codes of ethics—though how to apply such standards to citizen journalists is somewhat unclear. Ensuring journalists have a strong understanding of privacy issues and their rights is also important. Other education should be technical in nature, encouraging the use of antivirus software, trusted operating systems, encryption, and so on.

Respondents recognised interfaces between journalistic free expression and privacy, as signaled Resolution 52 of UNESCO's 37th General Conference in 2013: "privacy is essential to protect journalistic sources, which enable a society to benefit from investigative journalism, to strengthen good governance and the rule of law, and that such privacy should not be subject to arbitrary or unlawful interference." According to respondents, states have a duty to enact legislation and regulation that protects journalists, ideally according to standardized frameworks. This should be done democratically (through parliaments). Measures should include legal action against intimidating journalists, clear rules on a variety of topics (for instance, whistleblower protection; content moderation policies; when to contact authorities; content regulation, and narrowly defined rules where its removal is legitimate in terms of international standards; rules around proactive removal of content, and removal requests; and rules around the delivery of user information). Safe harbours for content, and co-regulation for ISPs, were also identified as possible solutions. In all cases, such regulation should have strong enforcement mechanisms to ensure compliance.

In addition, some respondents suggested journalistic self-regulation as a potentially viable alternative to state regulation. They argued that self-regulation would minimize state interference and preserve editorial freedom. However, some commentators expressed scepticism regarding the effectiveness of self-regulation, saying it might not work or might be undemocratic—or, potentially, even lead to self-censorship. Others suggested that journalistic unions or institutions, including press councils, are best-placed to establish regimes of self-regulation. Such organizations could be established at both the national and international levels.

### Regulatory Challenges: Hate Speech

Online hate speech has become an increasingly big problem for regulators, content platforms, and users themselves. Respondents diverged strongly on their suggested approaches to dealing with hate speech. A complexity is that it can be hard to clarify what exactly constitutes hate speech. International standards diverge as to whether "hatred" requires an incitement to harm, and what appropriate regulatory remedies might exist. Assessing whether a particular utterance in a given context amounts to the specific conception of hatred is a further complexity. Given the range of understandings, respondents cautioned that regulation should not prohibit legitimate political expression and criticism under the cloak of combatting hatred. Indeed, some respondents were in favour of a maximalist position, in which speech should be regulated as little as possible, with restrictions covering only the most important cases—such as the protection of children.

Respondents did not agree on whether online speech should be regulated less than offline speech, or whether existing rules and principles should be applied online. Views on prosecution were similarly diverse: some called for prosecution of the author, some for prosecution of the publisher, although it was not deeply addressed as to whether this included platforms of service providers who are not necessarily publishers in the traditional sense, and how this would impact on the principle of limited liability for Internet intermediaries. Other respondents pointed out that prosecution can have a chilling effect or be used as an excuse to eliminate legitimate speech and suggested it should be avoided altogether. Some respondents proposed that prosecution, if it occurs, should meet several tests, including not punishing statements of fact; only penalising those who are shown to have acted with the intent to incite; protecting journalism and reporting; and imposing punishment according to the principle of proportionality. Self-regulation by platform owners, via voluntary removal or moderation, was also identified as potentially valuable by quite a few respondents; but the caveats applying to self-regulation identified earlier in this section apply here, too. Finally, respondents disagreed about the effectiveness of "real name" policies: some saw them as beneficial, while others were concerned about the lack of anonymity they entail, and the potential for additional harassment.

Beyond regulation, a large number of respondents called for an increase in media and information literacy and education of the public. Ideally, this could shape behaviour by encouraging users to act with understanding and respect for others, and by reminding users that little said online is truly anonymous. Calling for "more speech," including offering more and better content, in response to trolling and hate speech, was also a popular response. Encouraging users to strengthen their sense of self, and to laugh at, counter or ridicule hateful speech, was also seen as an effective measure.

Finally, some respondents called for academic and multistakeholder exchanges on hate speech, including getting experts from civil society to help with identifying and effectively regulating hate speech online. Others pointed out that the media themselves need to play a role, and need funding to combat hate speech.

[...]

## Issues Related to Big Data

With the growth in the popularity of big data comes an increase in concerns about its collection, storage and use (see Mayer-Schönberger and Cukier 2013). There is controversy over how to define big data, but in essence the concept refers to very large data sets requiring advanced computational and networking technologies to capture and analyze. Examples would be a "firehose" of Twitter posts, or a database of records of phone calls. These can be codified and analyzed as big data to provide meaningful information. Social scientist, Daniel Bell (1973), once defined the "Information Society" as being driven by the ability to codify data to create information in ways that made the information sector as important as earlier agricultural and industrial sectors of the economy. The ways in which advanced computational and networking technologies enable the collection and analysis of data formerly perceived to be a problem—a data deluge—are examples of the power of codifying data. How to collect and manage this data ethically, and in ways that are truly informative and valid, is a subject of great controversy. One concern mentioned by respondents is that individuals often provide this data without realizing the purposes for which it might be used. Another is that by combining multiple, disparate data sets, anonymised data can become de-anonymised. Still another is that social decisions might increasingly be made based on data that does not sufficiently represent the diversity of communities—especially when issues of access and participation are not addressed. There is also concern over the security of storage in regard to hacking and misuse.

### Endnotes

1. This common example originated in 1919 with US Supreme Court Justice Oliver Wendell Holmes, Jr.'s opinion in the United States Supreme Court case *Schenck v. United States*.
2. Posetti et al. 2015

## Periodical and Internet Sources Bibliography

*The following articles have been selected to supplement the diverse views presented in this chapter.*

Bart Cammaerts, "Social Media and Activism," The London School of Economics and Political Science, June 2015. http://eprints.lse .ac.uk/62090/1/Social_media_and.pdf.

Luciano Floridi, "Fake News and a 400-Year-Old Problem: We Need to Resolve the 'Post-Truth' Crisis," *Guardian*, November 29, 2016. https://www.theguardian.com/technology/2016/nov/29/fake -news-echo-chamber-ethics-infosphere-internet-digital.

Jim Fruchterman, "We Need a Software Revolution for the Greater Social Good," Recode, March 22, 2017. http://www.recode .net/2017/3/22/15011658/social-sector-technology -entrepreneurs-philanthropy-investment.

Jodi Kantor and David Streitfeld, "Inside Amazon: Wrestling Big Ideas in a Bruising Workplace," *New York Times*, August 15, 2015. https://www.nytimes.com/2015/08/16/technology/inside -amazon-wrestling-big-ideas-in-a-bruising-workplace.html.

Kevin Maney, "Why Silicon Valley Should Create a 'Smart' Political Party," *Newsweek*, November 11, 2016. http://www.newsweek .com/silicon-valley-smart-political-party-519891.

George Packer, "Cheap Words," *New Yorker*, February 2014. http:// www.newyorker.com/magazine/2014/02/17/cheap-words.

Anna Wiener, "It's Getting Harder to Believe in Silicon Valley," *Atlantic*, March 2017. https://www.theatlantic.com/magazine /archive/2017/03/the-shine-comes-off-silicon-valley/513815.

Julia Carrie Wong, "Tech's 'Feel-Good' Promises: Why Silicon Valley's Charity Isn't Enough," Salon, February 19, 2014. http://www .salon.com/2014/02/19/the_tech_industrys_empty_promises_ why_silicon_valleys_charity_isnt_enough.

GLOBALVIEWPOINTS

# CHAPTER 4

# Are We Headed for a Technocracy?

# Technology Is Both Extending and Challenging the Foundations of Democracy

*Pia Waugh*

*In the following viewpoint, Pia Waugh surveys the historical overlap between technology and politics. A technocracy, as defined by Merriam Webster, is "a system in which people with a lot of knowledge about science or technology control a society." Waugh draws on theorists like Thomas Hobbes and John Locke, as well as the Declaration of Independence and the Universal Declaration of Human Rights, to establish precepts of democracy and social equality. She then examines prominent social structures—publishing, communications, monitoring, and enforcement—where technology cannons into bureaucracy. Waugh is director of coordination and Gov 2.0 in the Technology and Procurement Division of Finance for the Australian Government.*

As you read, consider the following questions:

1. How did Thomas Hobbes and John Locke differ in their view of government's purpose?
2. What is the panopticon and how does it fit into Foucault's theory of surveillance?
3. Why, in 2003, was the Salam Pax blog significant?

"Technocracy: A Short Look at the Impact of Technology on Modern Political and Power Structures," by Pipka, Pipka.org, March 8, 2015. Reprinted by permission.

I n recent centuries we have seen a dramatic change in the world brought about by the rise of and proliferation of modern democracies. This shift in governance structures gives the common individual a specific role in the power structure, and differs sharply from more traditional top down power structures. This change has instilled in many of the world's population some common assumptions about the roles, responsibilities and rights of citizens and their governing bodies. Though there will always exist a natural tension between those in power and those governed, modern governments are generally expected to be a benevolent and accountable mechanism that balances this tension for the good of the society as a whole.

In recent *decades* the Internet has rapidly further evolved the expectations and individual capacity of people around the globe through, for the first time in history, the mass distribution of the traditional bastions of power. With a third of the world online and countries starting to enshrine access to the Internet as a human right, individuals have more power than ever before to influence and shape their lives and the lives of people around them. It is easier that ever for people to congregate, albeit virtually, according to common interests and goals, regardless of their location, beliefs, language, culture or other age old barriers to collaboration. This is having a direct and dramatic impact on governments and traditional power structures everywhere, and is both extending and challenging the principles and foundations of democracy.

This short paper outlines how the Internet has empowered individuals in an unprecedented and prolific way, and how this has changed and continues to change the balance of power in societies around the world, including how governments and democracies work.

## Democracy and Equality

The concept of an individual having any implicit rights or equality isn't new, let alone the idea that an individual in a society should have some say over the ruling of the society. Indeed the idea of democracy itself has been around since the ancient Greeks in 500 BCE. The basis for modern democracies lies with the Parliament of England in the 11th century at a time when the laws of the Crown largely relied upon the support of the clergy and nobility, and the Great Council was formed for consultation and to gain consent from power brokers. In subsequent centuries, great concerns about leadership and taxes effectively led to a strongly increased role in administrative power and oversight by the parliament rather than the Crown.

The practical basis for modern government structures with elected official had emerged by the 17th century. This idea was already established in England, but also took root in the United States. This was closely followed by multiple suffrage movements from the 19th and 20th centuries which expanded the right to participate in modern democracies from (typically) adult white property owners to almost all adults in those societies.

It is quite astounding to consider the dramatic change from very hierarchical, largely unaccountable and highly centralised power systems to democratic ones in which those in powers are expected to be held to account. This shift from top down power, to distributed, representative and accountable power is an important step to understand modern expectations.

Democracy itself is sustainable only when the key principle of equality is deeply ingrained in the population at large. This principle has been largely infused into Western culture and democracies, independent of religion, including in largely secular and multicultural democracies such as Australia. This is important because an assumption of equality underpins stability in a system that puts into the hands of its citizens the ability to make a decision. If one component of the society feels another doesn't have an equal right to a vote, then outcomes other than their own are not accepted as legitimate. This has been an ongoing challenge in some parts of the world more than others.

In many ways there is a huge gap between the fearful sentiments of Thomas Hobbes, who preferred a complete and powerful authority to keep the supposed "brutish nature" of mankind at bay, and the aspirations of John Locke who felt that even governments should be held to account and the role of the government was to secure the natural rights of the individual to life, liberty and property. Yet both of these men and indeed, many political theorists over many years, have started from a premise that all men are equal—either equally capable of taking from and harming others, or equal with regards to their individual rights.

Arguably, the Western notion of individual rights is rooted in religion. The Christian idea that all men are created equal under a deity presents an interesting contrast to traditional power structures that assume one person, family or group have more rights than the rest, although ironically various churches have not treated all people equally either. Christianity has deeply influenced many political thinkers and the forming of modern democracies, many of which which look very similar to the mixed regime system described by Saint Thomas Aquinas in his *Summa Thelogiae* essays:

> Some, indeed, say that the best constitution is a combination of all existing forms, and they praise the Lacedemonian because it is made up of oligarchy, monarchy, and democracy, the king forming the monarchy, and the council of elders the oligarchy, while the democratic element is represented by the Ephors: for the Ephors are selected from the people.

The assumption of equality has been enshrined in key influential documents including the United States Declaration of Independence, 1776:

> We hold these truths to be self-evident, that all men are created equal, that they are endowed by their Creator with certain unalienable Rights, that among these are Life, Liberty and the pursuit of Happiness.

More recently in the 20th Century, the Universal Declaration of Human Rights goes even further to define and enshrine equality and rights, marking them as important for the entire society:

> Whereas recognition of the inherent dignity and of the equal and inalienable rights of all members of the human family is the foundation of freedom, justice and peace in the world…
> — 1st sentence of the Preamble to the Universal Declaration of Human Rights
>
> All human beings are born free and equal in dignity and rights. — Article 1 of the United Nations Universal Declaration of Human Rights (UDHR)

The evolution of the concepts of equality and "rights" is important to understand as they provide the basis for how the Internet is having such a disruptive impact on traditional power structures, whilst also being a natural extension of an evolution in human thinking that has been hundreds of years in the making.

## Great Expectations

Although only a third of the world is online, in many countries this means the vast bulk of the population. In Australia over 88% of households are online as of 2012. Constant online access starts to drive a series of new expectations and behaviours in a community, especially one where equality has already been so deeply ingrained as a basic principle.

Over time a series of Internet-based instincts and perspectives have become mainstream, arguably driven by the very nature of the technology and the tools that we use online. For example, the Internet was developed to "route around damage" which means the technology can withstand technical interruption by another hardware or software means. Where damage is interpreted in a social sense, such as perhaps censorship or locking away access to knowledge, individuals instinctively seek and develop a work around and you see something quite profound. A society has emerged that doesn't blindly accept limitations put upon them. This is quite a challenge for traditional power structures.

The Internet has become both an extension and an enabler of equality and power by massively distributing both to ordinary people around the world. How has power and equality been distributed? When you consider what constitutes power, four elements come to mind: publishing, communications, monitoring and enforcement.

Publishing—in times gone past the ideas that spread beyond a small geographical area either traveled word of mouth via trade routes, or made it into a book. Only the wealthy could afford to print and distribute the written word, so publishing and dissemination of information was a power limited to a small number of people. Today the spreading of ideas is extremely easy, cheap and can be done anonymously. Anyone can start a blog, use social media, and the proliferation of information creation and dissemination is unprecedented. How does this change society? Firstly there is an assumption that an individual can tell their story to a global audience, which means an official story is easily challenged not only by the intended audience, but by the people about whom the story is written. Individuals online expect both to have their say, and to find multiple perspectives that they can weigh up, and determine for themselves what is most credible. This presents significant challenges to traditional powers such as governments in establishing an authoritative voice unless they can establish trust with the citizens they serve.

Communications—individuals have always had some method to communicate with individuals in other communities and countries, but up until recent decades these methods have been quite expensive, slow and oftentimes controlled. This has meant that historically, people have tended to form social and professional relationships with those close by, largely out of convenience. The Internet has made it easy to communicate, collaborate with, and coordinate with individuals and groups all around the world, in real time. This has made massive and global civil responses and movements possible, which has challenged traditional and geographically defined powers substantially. It has also presented a significant challenge for governments to predict and control information flow and relationships within the society. It also created a challenge for how to support the best interests of citizens, given the tension between what is good for a geographically defined nation state doesn't always align with what is good for an online and trans-nationally focused citizen.

Monitoring—traditional power structures have always had ways to monitor the masses. Monitoring helps maintain rule of law through assisting in the enforcement of laws, and is often upheld through self-reporting as those affected by broken laws will report issues to hold detractors to account. In just the last 50 years, modern technologies like CCTV have made monitoring of the people a trivial task, where video cameras can record what is happening 24 hours a day. Foucault spoke of the panopticon gaol design as a metaphor for a modern surveillance state, where everyone is constantly watched on camera. The panopticon was a gaol design wherein detainees could not tell if they were being observed by gaolers or not, enabling in principle, less gaolers to control a large number of prisoners. In the same way prisoners would theoretically behave better under observation, Foucault was concerned that omnipresent surveillance would lead to all individuals being more conservative and limited in themselves if they knew they could be watched at any time. The Internet has turned this model on its head. Although governments can more easily monitor citizens than ever before, individuals can also monitor each other and indeed, monitor governments for misbehaviour. This has led to individuals, governments, companies and other entities all being held to account publicly, sometimes violently or unfairly so.

Enforcement—enforcement of laws are a key role of a power structure, to ensure the rules of a society are maintained for the benefit of stability and prosperity. Enforcement can take many forms including physical (gaol, punishment) or psychological (pressure, public humiliation). Power structures have many ways of enforcing the rules of a society on individuals, but the Internet gives individuals substantial enforcement tools of their own. Power used to be who had the biggest sword, or gun, or police force. Now that major powers and indeed, economies, rely so heavily upon the Internet, there is a power in the ability to disrupt communications. In taking down a government or corporate website or online service, an individual or small group of individuals can have an impact far greater than in the past on power structures in their society, and can do so anonymously. This becomes quite profound as citizen groups can emerge with their own philosophical premise and the tools to monitor and enforce their perspective.

Property—property has always been a strong basis of law and order and still plays an important part in democracy, though perspectives towards property are arguably starting to shift. Copyright was invented to protect the "intellectual property" of a person against copying at a time when copying was quite a physical business, and when the mode of distributing information was very expensive. Now, digital information is so easy to copy that it has created a change in expectations and a struggle for traditional models of intellectual property. New models of copyright have emerged that explicitly support copying (copyleft) and some have been successful, such as with the Open Source software industry or with remix music culture. 3D printing will change the game again as we will see in the near future the massive distribution of the ability to copy physical goods, not just virtual ones. This is already creating havoc with those who seek to protect traditional approaches to property but it also presents an extraordinary opportunity for mankind to have greater distribution of physical wealth, not just virtual wealth. Particularly if you consider the current use of 3D printing to create transplant organs, or the potential of 3D printing combined with some form of nano technology that could reassemble matter into food or other essential living items. That is starting to step into science fiction, but we should consider the broader potential of these new technologies before we decide to arbitrarily limit them based on traditional views of copyright, as we are already starting to see.

By massively distributing publishing, communications, monitoring and enforcement, and with the coming potential massive distribution of property, technology and the Internet has created an ad hoc, self-determined and grassroots power base that challenges traditional power structures and governments.

## With Great Power...

Individuals online find themselves more empowered and self-determined than ever before, regardless of the socio-political nature of their circumstances. They can share and seek information directly from other individuals, bypassing traditional gatekeepers of knowledge. They can coordinate with like-minded citizens both nationally and internationally and establish communities of interest that transcend geo-politics. They can monitor elected officials, bureaucrats, companies and other individuals, and even hold them all to account.

To leverage these opportunities fully requires a reasonable amount of technical literacy. As such, many technologists are on the front line, playing a special role in supporting, challenging and sometimes overthrowing modern power structures. As technical literacy is permeating mainstream culture more individuals are able to leverage these disrupters, but technologist activists are often the most effective at disrupting power through the use of technology and the Internet.

Of course, whilst the Internet is a threat to traditional centralised power structures, it also presents an unprecedented opportunity to leverage the skills, knowledge and efforts of an entire society in the running of government, for the benefit of all. Citizen engagement in democracy and government beyond the ballot box presents the ability to co-develop, or co-design the future of the society, including the services and rules that support stability and prosperity. Arguably, citizen buy-in and support is now an important part of the stability of a society and success of a policy.

## Disrupting the Status Quo

The combination of improved capacity for self-determination by individuals along with the increasingly pervasive assumptions of equality and rights have led to many examples of traditional power structures being held to account, challenged, and in some cases, overthrown.

Governments are able to be held more strongly to account than ever before. The Open Australia Foundation is a small group of technologists in Australia who create tools to improve transparency and citizen engagement in the Australian democracy. They created Open Australia, a site that made the public parliamentary record more accessible to individuals through making it searchable, subscribable and easy to browse and comment on. They also have projects such as Planning Alerts which notifies citizens of planned development in their area, Election Leaflets where citizens upload political pamphlets for public record and accountability, and Right to Know, a site to assist the general public in pursuing information and public records from the government under Freedom of Information. These are all projects that monitor, engage and inform citizens about government.

Wikileaks is a website and organisation that provides an anonymous way for individuals to anonymously leak sensitive information, often classified government information. Key examples include video and documents from the Iraq and Afghanistan wars, about the Guantanamo Bay detention camp, United States diplomatic cables and million of emails from Syrian political and corporate figures. Some of the information revealed by Wikileaks has had quite dramatic consequences with the media and citizens around the world responding to the information. Arguably, many of the Arab Spring uprisings throughout the Middle East from December 2010 were provoked by the release of the US diplomatic cables by Wikileaks, as it demonstrated very clearly the level of corruption in many countries. The Internet also played a vital part in many of these uprisings, some of which saw governments deposed, as social media tools such as Twitter and

Facebook provided the mechanism for massive coordination of protests, but importantly also provided a way to get citizen coverage of the protests and police/army brutality, creating global audience, commentary and pressure on the governments and support for the protesters.

Citizen journalism is an interesting challenge to governments because the route to communicate with the general public has traditionally been through the media. The media has presented for many years a reasonably predictable mechanism for governments to communicate an official statement and shape public narrative. But the Internet has facilitated any individual to publish online to a global audience, and this has resulted in a much more robust exchange of ideas and less clear cut public narrative about any particular issue, sometimes directly challenging official statements. A particularly interesting case of this was the Salam Pax blog during the 2003 Iraq invasion by the United States. Official news from the US would largely talk about the success of the campaign to overthrown Suddam Hussein. The Salam Pax blog provided the view of a 29 year old educated Iraqi architect living in Baghdad and experiencing the invasion as a citizen, which contrasted quite significantly at times with official US Government reports. This type of contrast will continue to be a challenge to governments.

On the flip side, the Internet has also provided new ways for governments themselves to support and engage citizens. There has been the growth of a global open government movement, where governments themselves try to improve transparency, public engagement and services delivery using the Internet. Open data is a good example of this, with governments going above and beyond traditional freedom of information obligations to proactively release raw data online for public scrutiny. Digital services allow citizens to interact with their government online rather than the inconvenience of having to physically attend a shopfront. Many governments around the world are making public commitments to improving the transparency, engagement and services for their citizens. We now also see more politicians and bureaucrats engaging directly with citizens online through the use of social media, blogs and sophisticated public consultations tools. Governments have become, in short, more engaged, more responsive and more accountable to more people than ever before.

## Conclusion

Only in recent centuries have power structures emerged with a specific role for common individual citizens. The relationship between individuals and power structures has long been about the balance between what the power could enforce and what the population would accept. With the emergence of power structures that support and enshrine the principles of equality and human rights, individuals around the world have come to expect the capacity to determine their own future. The growth of and proliferation of democracy has been a key shift in how individuals relate to power and governance structures.

New technologies and the Internet has gone on to massively distribute the traditionally centralised powers of publishing, communications, monitoring and enforcement (with property on the way). This distribution of power through the means of technology has seen democracy evolve into something of a technocracy, a system which has effectively tipped the balance of power from institutions to individuals.

*References*
Hobbes, T. *The Leviathan*, ed. by R. Tuck, Cambridge University Press, 1991.
Aquinas, T. *Sum. Theol.* i-ii. 105. 1, trans. A. C. Pegis, *Whether the old law enjoined fitting precepts concerning rulers?*
Uzgalis, William, "John Locke", The Stanford Encyclopedia of Philosophy (Fall 2012 Edition), Edward N. Zalta (ed.), http://plato.stanford.edu/archives/fall2012/entries/locke/.

# Rather Than Fearing Artificial Intelligence, We Should Drive It

*Max Tegmark*

*In the following viewpoint, Max Tegmark, spurred by public statements of concern made by Elon Musk, Bill Gates, Stephen Hawking, and other techno-luminaries regarding artificial intelligence, unpacks some of the myths that attend AI. Much of Tegmark's focus has to do with consciousness, which he believes is irrelevant when it comes to robots because machines are goal-oriented. "The main concern of the beneficial-AI movement," he writes, "isn't with robots but with intelligence itself: specifically, intelligence whose goals are misaligned with ours." Tegmark is a professor at the Massachusetts Institute of Technology and cofounder of the Future of Life Institute, which studies the existential threats posed by AI.*

As you read, consider the following questions:

1. What is the difference between weak and strong AI?
2. Why does Tegmark advocate starting AI safety research now, even if human-level AI is not yet a reality?
3. What relationship does Tegmark propose between intelligence and goal-attainment?

> *"Everything we love about civilization is a product of intelligence, so amplifying our human intelligence with artificial intelligence has the potential of helping civilization flourish like never before—as long as we manage to keep the technology beneficial."*
> Max Tegmark, President of the Future of Life Institute

## What Is AI?

From SIRI to self-driving cars, artificial intelligence (AI) is progressing rapidly. While science fiction often portrays AI as robots with human-like characteristics, AI can encompass anything from Google's search algorithms to IBM's Watson to autonomous weapons.

Artificial intelligence today is properly known as narrow AI (or weak AI), in that it is designed to perform a narrow task (e.g. only facial recognition or only internet searches or only driving a car). However, the long-term goal of many researchers is to create general AI (AGI or strong AI). While narrow AI may outperform humans at whatever its specific task is, like playing chess or solving equations, AGI would outperform humans at nearly every cognitive task.

## Why Research AI Safety?

In the near term, the goal of keeping AI's impact on society beneficial motivates research in many areas, from economics and law to technical topics such as verification, validity, security and control. Whereas it may be little more than a minor nuisance if your laptop crashes or gets hacked, it becomes all the more important that an AI system does what you want it to do if it controls your car, your airplane, your pacemaker, your automated trading system or your power grid. Another short-term challenge is preventing a devastating arms race in lethal autonomous weapons.

In the long term, an important question is what will happen if the quest for strong AI succeeds and an AI system becomes better than humans at all cognitive tasks. As pointed out by I.J. Good in 1965, designing smarter AI systems is itself a cognitive task. Such a system could potentially undergo recursive self-improvement, triggering an intelligence explosion leaving human intellect far behind. By inventing revolutionary new technologies, such a superintelligence might help us eradicate war, disease, and poverty, and so the creation of strong AI might be the biggest event in human history. Some experts have expressed concern, though, that it might also be the last, unless we learn to align the goals of the AI with ours before it becomes superintelligent.

There are some who question whether strong AI will ever be achieved, and others who insist that the creation of superintelligent AI is guaranteed to be beneficial. At FLI we recognize both of these possibilities, but also recognize the potential for an artificial intelligence system to intentionally or unintentionally cause great harm. We believe research today will help us better prepare for and prevent such potentially negative consequences in the future, thus enjoying the benefits of AI while avoiding pitfalls.

## How Can AI Be Dangerous?

Most researchers agree that a superintelligent AI is unlikely to exhibit human emotions like love or hate, and that there is no reason to expect AI to become intentionally benevolent or malevolent. Instead, when considering how AI might become a risk, experts think two scenarios most likely:

**The AI is programmed to do something devastating:** Autonomous weapons are artificial intelligence systems that are programmed to kill. In the hands of the wrong person, these weapons could easily cause mass casualties. Moreover, an AI arms race could inadvertently lead to an AI war that also results in mass casualties. To avoid being thwarted by the enemy, these weapons would be designed to be extremely difficult to simply "turn off," so humans could plausibly lose control of such a situation. This risk is one that's present even with narrow AI, but grows as levels of AI intelligence and autonomy increase.

**The AI is programmed to do something beneficial, but it develops a destructive method for achieving its goal:** This can happen whenever we fail to fully align the AI's goals with ours, which is strikingly difficult. If you ask an obedient intelligent car to take you to the airport as fast as possible, it might get you there chased by helicopters and covered in vomit, doing not what you wanted but literally what you asked for. If a superintelligent system is tasked with a ambitious geoengineering project, it might wreak havoc with our ecosystem as a side effect, and view human attempts to stop it as a threat to be met.

As these examples illustrate, the concern about advanced AI isn't malevolence but competence. A super-intelligent AI will be extremely good at accomplishing its goals, and if those goals aren't aligned with ours, we have a problem. You're probably not an evil ant-hater who steps on ants out of malice, but if you're in charge of a hydroelectric green energy project and there's an anthill in the region to be flooded, too bad for the ants. A key goal of AI safety research is to never place humanity in the position of those ants.

## Why the Recent Interest in AI Safety

Stephen Hawking, Elon Musk, Steve Wozniak, Bill Gates, and many other big names in science and technology have recently expressed concern in the media and via open letters about the risks posed by AI, joined by many leading AI researchers. Why is the subject suddenly in the headlines?

The idea that the quest for strong AI would ultimately succeed was long thought of as science fiction, centuries or more away. However, thanks to recent breakthroughs, many AI milestones, which experts viewed as decades away merely five years ago, have now been reached, making many experts take seriously the possibility of superintelligence in our lifetime. While some experts still guess that human-level AI is centuries away, most AI researches at the 2015 Puerto Rico Conference guessed that it would happen before 2060. Since it may take decades to complete the required safety research, it is prudent to start it now.

Because AI has the potential to become more intelligent than any human, we have no surefire way of predicting how it will behave. We can't use past technological developments as much of a basis because we've never created anything that has the ability to, wittingly or unwittingly, outsmart us. The best example of what we could face may be our own evolution. People now control the planet, not because we're the strongest, fastest or biggest, but because we're the smartest. If we're no longer the smartest, are we assured to remain in control?

FLI's position is that our civilization will flourish as long as we win the race between the growing power of technology and the wisdom with which we manage it. In the case of AI technology, FLI's position is that the best way to win that race is not to impede the former, but to accelerate the latter, by supporting AI safety research.

## The Top Myths About Advanced AI

A captivating conversation is taking place about the future of artificial intelligence and what it will/should mean for humanity. There are fascinating controversies where the world's leading experts disagree, such as: AI's future impact on the job market; if/when human-level AI will be developed; whether this will lead to an intelligence explosion; and whether this is something we should welcome or fear. But there are also many examples of of boring pseudo-controversies caused by people misunderstanding and talking past each other. To help ourselves focus on the interesting controversies and open questions—and not on the misunderstandings—let's clear up some of the most common myths.

| | |
|---|---|
| **Myth:** Superintelligence by 2100 is inevitable<br>**Myth:** Superintelligence by 2100 is impossible | **Fact:** It may happen in decades, centuries, or never: AI experts disagree & we simply don't know |
| **Myth:** Only Luddites worry about AI | **Fact:** Many top AI researchers are concerned |
| **Mythical worry:** AI turning evil<br>**Mythical worry:** AI turning conscious | **Actual worry:** AI turning competent, with goals misaligned with ours |
| **Myth:** Robots are the main concern | **Fact:** Misaligned intelligence is the main concern: it needs no body, only an internet connection |
| **Myth:** AI can't control humans | **Fact:** Intelligence enables control: we control tigers by being smarter |
| **Myth:** Machines can't have goals | **Fact:** A heat-seeking missile has a goal |
| **Mythical worry:** Superintelligence is just years away | **Actual worry:** It's at least decades away, but it may take that long to make it safe |

## Timeline Myths

The first myth regards the timeline: how long will it take until machines greatly supersede human-level intelligence? A common misconception is that we know the answer with great certainly.

One popular myth is that we know we'll get superhuman AI this century. In fact, history is full of technological over-hyping. Where are those fusion power plants and flying cars we were promised we'd have by now? AI has also been repeatedly over-hyped in the past, even by some of the founders of the field. For example, John McCarthy (who coined the term "artificial intelligence"), Marvin Minsky, Nathaniel Rochester and Claude Shannon wrote this overly optimistic forecast about what could be accomplished during two months with stone-age computers: *"We propose that a 2 month, 10 man study of artificial intelligence be carried out during the summer of 1956 at Dartmouth College [...] An attempt will be made to find how to make machines use language, form abstractions and concepts, solve kinds of problems now reserved for humans, and improve themselves. We think that a significant advance can be made in one or more of these problems if a carefully selected group of scientists work on it together for a summer."*

On the other hand, a popular counter-myth is that we know we won't get superhuman AI this century. Researchers have made a wide range of estimates for how far we are from superhuman AI, but we certainly can't say with great confidence that the probability is zero this century, given the dismal track record of such techno-skeptic predictions. For example, Ernest Rutherford, arguably the greatest nuclear physicist of his time, said in 1933—less than 24 hours before Szilard's invention of the nuclear chain reaction—that nuclear energy was "moonshine." And Astronomer Royal Richard Woolley called interplanetary travel "utter bilge" in 1956. The most extreme form of this myth is that superhuman AI will never arrive because it's physically impossible. However, physicists know that a brain consists of quarks and electrons arranged to act as a powerful computer, and that there's no law of physics preventing us from building even more intelligent quark blobs.

There have been a number of surveys asking AI researchers how many years from now they think we'll have human-level AI with at least 50% probability. All these surveys have the same conclusion: the world's leading experts disagree, so we simply don't know. For example, in such a poll of the AI researchers at the 2015 Puerto Rico AI conference, the average (median) answer was by year 2045, but some researchers guessed hundreds of years or more.

There's also a related myth that people who worry about AI think it's only a few years away. In fact, most people on record worrying about superhuman AI guess it's still at least decades away. But they argue that as long as we're not 100% sure that it won't happen this century, it's smart to start safety research now to prepare for the eventuality. Many of the safety problems associated with human-level AI are so hard that they may take decades to solve. So it's prudent to start researching them now rather than the night before some programmers drinking Red Bull decide to switch one on.

## Controversy Myths

Another common misconception is that the only people harboring concerns about AI and advocating AI safety research are luddites who don't know much about AI. When Stuart Russell, author of the standard AI textbook, mentioned this during his Puerto Rico talk, the audience laughed loudly. A related misconception is that supporting AI safety research is hugely controversial. In fact, to support a modest investment in AI safety research, people don't need to be convinced that risks are high, merely non-negligible—just as a modest investment in home insurance is justified by a non-negligible probability of the home burning down.

It may be that media have made the AI safety debate seem more controversial than it really is. After all, fear sells, and articles using out-of-context quotes to proclaim imminent doom can generate more clicks than nuanced and balanced ones. As a result, two people who only know about each other's positions from media quotes are likely to think they disagree more than they really do.

For example, a techno-skeptic who only read about Bill Gates's position in a British tabloid may mistakenly think Gates believes superintelligence to be imminent. Similarly, someone in the beneficial-AI movement who knows nothing about Andrew Ng's position except his quote about overpopulation on Mars may mistakenly think he doesn't care about AI safety, whereas in fact, he does. The crux is simply that because Ng's timeline estimates are longer, he naturally tends to prioritize short-term AI challenges over long-term ones.

## Myths About the Risks of Superhuman AI

Many AI researchers roll their eyes when seeing this headline: *"Stephen Hawking warns that rise of robots may be disastrous for mankind."* And as many have lost count of how many similar articles they've seen. Typically, these articles are accompanied by an evil-looking robot carrying a weapon, and they suggest we should worry about robots rising up and killing us because they've become conscious and/or evil. On a lighter note, such articles are actually rather impressive, because they succinctly summarize the scenario that AI researchers don't worry about. That scenario combines as many as three separate misconceptions: concern about consciousness, evil, and robots.

If you drive down the road, you have a subjective experience of colors, sounds, etc. But does a self-driving car have a subjective experience? Does it feel like anything at all to be a self-driving car? Although this mystery of consciousness is interesting in its own right, it's irrelevant to AI risk. If you get struck by a driverless car, it makes no difference to you whether it subjectively feels conscious. In the same way, what will affect us humans is what superintelligent AI *does*, not how it subjectively *feels*.

The fear of machines turning evil is another red herring. The real worry isn't malevolence, but competence. A superintelligent AI is by definition very good at attaining its goals, whatever they may be, so we need to ensure that its goals are aligned with ours.

Humans don't generally hate ants, but we're more intelligent than they are—so if we want to build a hydroelectric dam and there's an anthill there, too bad for the ants. The beneficial-AI movement wants to avoid placing humanity in the position of those ants.

The consciousness misconception is related to the myth that machines can't have goals. Machines can obviously have goals in the narrow sense of exhibiting goal-oriented behavior: the behavior of a heat-seeking missile is most economically explained as a goal to hit a target. If you feel threatened by a machine whose goals are misaligned with yours, then it is precisely its goals in this narrow sense that troubles you, not whether the machine is conscious and experiences a sense of purpose. If that heat-seeking missile were chasing you, you probably wouldn't exclaim: *"I'm not worried, because machines can't have goals!"*

I sympathize with Rodney Brooks and other robotics pioneers who feel unfairly demonized by scaremongering tabloids, because some journalists seem obsessively fixated on robots and adorn many of their articles with evil-looking metal monsters with red shiny eyes. In fact, the main concern of the beneficial-AI movement isn't with robots but with intelligence itself: specifically, intelligence whose goals are misaligned with ours. To cause us trouble, such misaligned superhuman intelligence needs no robotic body, merely an internet connection—this may enable outsmarting financial markets, out-inventing human researchers, out-manipulating human leaders, and developing weapons we cannot even understand. Even if building robots were physically impossible, a super-intelligent and super-wealthy AI could easily pay or manipulate many humans to unwittingly do its bidding.

The robot misconception is related to the myth that machines can't control humans. Intelligence enables control: humans control tigers not because we are stronger, but because we are smarter. This means that if we cede our position as smartest on our planet, it's possible that we might also cede control.

## The Interesting Controversies

Not wasting time on the above-mentioned misconceptions lets us focus on true and interesting controversies where even the experts disagree. What sort of future do you want? Should we develop lethal autonomous weapons? What would you like to happen with job automation? What career advice would you give today's kids? Do you prefer new jobs replacing the old ones, or a jobless society where everyone enjoys a life of leisure and machine-produced wealth? Further down the road, would you like us to create superintelligent life and spread it through our cosmos? Will we control intelligent machines or will they control us? Will intelligent machines replace us, coexist with us, or merge with us? What will it mean to be human in the age of artificial intelligence? What would you like it to mean, and how can we make the future be that way? Please join the conversation!

# Now Is the Time to Decide What to Do with Artificial Intelligence

*Julia Bossmann*

*In the following viewpoint, Julia Bossmann investigates nine economic, ethical, and cultural challenges posed by artificial intelligence. Will machines displace the bulk of the human workforce? What will humans do then? What to do about biased AI? Who will make these policy decisions? Should robots have rights? Her inquiries shed light on the essential dilemmas posed by a rapidly advancing, and potentially pernicious, technology. Bossmann is president of the Foresight Institute, a think tank focused on issues related to AI, nanotechnology, and biotech.*

As you read, consider the following questions:

1. How might AI increase income equality?
2. What is the Turing challenge?
3. What are "generic algorithms" and why are they significant?

Optimizing logistics, detecting fraud, composing art, conducting research, providing translations: intelligent machine systems are transforming our lives for the better. As these systems become more capable, our world becomes more efficient and consequently richer.

"Top 9 Ethical Issues in Artificial Intelligence," by Julia Bossmann, World Economic Forum, October 21, 2016. Reprinted by permission.

Tech giants such as Alphabet, Amazon, Facebook, IBM and Microsoft—as well as individuals like Stephen Hawking and Elon Musk—believe that now is the right time to talk about the nearly boundless landscape of artificial intelligence. In many ways, this is just as much a new frontier for ethics and risk assessment as it is for emerging technology. So which issues and conversations keep AI experts up at night?

## 1. Unemployment. What happens after the end of jobs?

The hierarchy of labour is concerned primarily with automation. As we've invented ways to automate jobs, we could create room for people to assume more complex roles, moving from the physical work that dominated the pre-industrial globe to the cognitive labour that characterizes strategic and administrative work in our globalized society.

Look at trucking: it currently employs millions of individuals in the United States alone. What will happen to them if the self-driving trucks promised by Tesla's Elon Musk become widely available in the next decade? But on the other hand, if we consider the lower risk of accidents, self-driving trucks seem like an ethical choice. The same scenario could happen to office workers, as well as to the majority of the workforce in developed countries.

This is where we come to the question of how we are going to spend our time. Most people still rely on selling their time to have enough income to sustain themselves and their families. We can only hope that this opportunity will enable people to find meaning in non-labour activities, such as caring for their families, engaging with their communities and learning new ways to contribute to human society.

If we succeed with the transition, one day we might look back and think that it was barbaric that human beings were required to sell the majority of their waking time just to be able to live.

## 2. Inequality. How do we distribute the wealth created by machines?

Our economic system is based on compensation for contribution to the economy, often assessed using an hourly wage. The majority of companies are still dependent on hourly work when it comes to products and services. But by using artificial intelligence, a company can drastically cut down on relying on the human workforce, and this means that revenues will go to fewer people. Consequently, individuals who have ownership in AI-driven companies will make all the money.

We are already seeing a widening wealth gap, where start-up founders take home a large portion of the economic surplus they create. In 2014, roughly the same revenues were generated by the three biggest companies in Detroit and the three biggest companies in Silicon Valley ... only in Silicon Valley there were 10 times fewer employees.

If we're truly imagining a post-work society, how do we structure a fair post-labour economy?

## 3. Humanity. How do machines affect our behaviour and interaction?

Artificially intelligent bots are becoming better and better at modelling human conversation and relationships. In 2015, a bot named Eugene Goostman won the Turing Challenge for the first time. In this challenge, human raters used text input to chat with an unknown entity, then guessed whether they had been chatting with a human or a machine. Eugene Goostman fooled more than half of the human raters into thinking they had been talking to a human being.

This milestone is only the start of an age where we will frequently interact with machines as if they are humans; whether in customer service or sales. While humans are limited in the attention and kindness that they can expend on another person, artificial bots can channel virtually unlimited resources into building relationships.

Even though not many of us are aware of this, we are already witnesses to how machines can trigger the reward centres in the human brain. Just look at click-bait headlines and video games. These headlines are often optimized with A/B testing, a rudimentary form of algorithmic optimization for content to capture our attention. This and other methods are used to make numerous video and mobile games become addictive. Tech addiction is the new frontier of human dependency.

On the other hand, maybe we can think of a different use for software, which has already become effective at directing human attention and triggering certain actions. When used right, this could evolve into an opportunity to nudge society towards more beneficial behavior. However, in the wrong hands it could prove detrimental.

## 4. Artificial stupidity. How can we guard against mistakes?

Intelligence comes from learning, whether you're human or machine. Systems usually have a training phase in which they "learn" to detect the right patterns and act according to their input. Once a system is fully trained, it can then go into test phase, where it is hit with more examples and we see how it performs.

Obviously, the training phase cannot cover all possible examples that a system may deal with in the real world. These systems can be fooled in ways that humans wouldn't be. For example, random dot patterns can lead a machine to "see" things that aren't there. If we rely on AI to bring us into a new world of labour, security and efficiency, we need to ensure that the machine performs as planned, and that people can't overpower it to use it for their own ends.

## 5. Racist robots. How do we eliminate AI bias?

Though artificial intelligence is capable of a speed and capacity of processing that's far beyond that of humans, it cannot always be trusted to be fair and neutral. Google and its parent company

Alphabet are one of the leaders when it comes to artificial intelligence, as seen in Google's Photos service, where AI is used to identify people, objects and scenes. But it can go wrong, such as when a camera missed the mark on racial sensitivity, or when a software used to predict future criminals showed bias against black people.

We shouldn't forget that AI systems are created by humans, who can be biased and judgemental. Once again, if used right, or if used by those who strive for social progress, artificial intelligence can become a catalyst for positive change.

## 6. Security. How do we keep AI safe from adversaries?

The more powerful a technology becomes, the more can it be used for nefarious reasons as well as good. This applies not only to robots produced to replace human soldiers, or autonomous weapons, but to AI systems that can cause damage if used maliciously. Because these fights won't be fought on the battleground only, cybersecurity will become even more important. After all, we're dealing with a system that is faster and more capable than us by orders of magnitude.

## 7. Evil genies. How do we protect against unintended consequences?

It's not just adversaries we have to worry about. What if artificial intelligence itself turned against us? This doesn't mean by turning "evil" in the way a human might, or the way AI disasters are depicted in Hollywood movies. Rather, we can imagine an advanced AI system as a "genie in a bottle" that can fulfill wishes, but with terrible unforeseen consequences.

In the case of a machine, there is unlikely to be malice at play, only a lack of understanding of the full context in which the wish was made. Imagine an AI system that is asked to eradicate cancer in the world. After a lot of computing, it spits out a formula that does, in fact, bring about the end of cancer—by killing everyone on the planet. The computer would have achieved its goal of "no more cancer" very efficiently, but not in the way humans intended it.

## 8. Singularity. How do we stay in control of a complex intelligent system?

The reason humans are on top of the food chain is not down to sharp teeth or strong muscles. Human dominance is almost entirely due to our ingenuity and intelligence. We can get the better of bigger, faster, stronger animals because we can create and use tools to control them: both physical tools such as cages and weapons, and cognitive tools like training and conditioning.

This poses a serious question about artificial intelligence: will it, one day, have the same advantage over us? We can't rely on just "pulling the plug" either, because a sufficiently advanced machine may anticipate this move and defend itself. This is what some call the "singularity": the point in time when human beings are no longer the most intelligent beings on earth.

## 9. Robot rights. How do we define the humane treatment of AI?

While neuroscientists are still working on unlocking the secrets of conscious experience, we understand more about the basic mechanisms of reward and aversion. We share these mechanisms with even simple animals. In a way, we are building similar mechanisms of reward and aversion in systems of artificial intelligence. For example, reinforcement learning is similar to training a dog: improved performance is reinforced with a virtual reward.

Right now, these systems are fairly superficial, but they are becoming more complex and life-like. Could we consider a system to be suffering when its reward functions give it negative input? What's more, so-called genetic algorithms work by creating many instances of a system at once, of which only the most successful "survive" and combine to form the next generation of instances.

This happens over many generations and is a way of improving a system. The unsuccessful instances are deleted. At what point might we consider genetic algorithms a form of mass murder?

Once we consider machines as entities that can perceive, feel and act, it's not a huge leap to ponder their legal status. Should they be treated like animals of comparable intelligence? Will we consider the suffering of "feeling" machines?

Some ethical questions are about mitigating suffering, some about risking negative outcomes. While we consider these risks, we should also keep in mind that, on the whole, this technological progress means better lives for everyone. Artificial intelligence has vast potential, and its responsible implementation is up to us.

# Public Safety Is More Important Than Corporate Loyalty

*Robert Merkel*

*In the following viewpoint, Robert Merkel asks how the Volkswagen scandal, in which the car company used a device to cheat emissions testing, could have happened. Because such high-cost machines are put through rigorous testing, Merkel argues, it is unlikely that errors were made by junior engineers and highly likely that deceit played a part. But where was the company whistleblower, standing fast to a code of ethics? Corporate loyalty should not trump public safety. Merkel is a lecturer in software engineering at Monash University.*

As you read, consider the following questions:

1. What are benchmarks?
2. Why is the author skeptical of Volkswagen's public statements regarding the incident?
3. Why are examples of whistleblowers among engineers so rare, according to the author?

The "defeat device" used by Volkswagen to cheat emissions testing in its diesel vehicles may be history's most costly software-related blunder.

"Where Were the Whistleblowers in the Volkswagen Emissions Scandal?" by Robert Merkel, The Conversation, September 29, 2015. https://theconversation.com/where-were-the-whistleblowers-in-the-volkswagen-emissions-scandal-48249.Licensed under CC BY-ND 4.0 International.

But why did nobody in the German car giant speak out when questions were raised over how it intended to use the engine management software in some of its engines?

As the Notice of Violation from the the United States Environmental Protection Agency (EPA) explains, the software in Volkswagen's EA189 diesel engines detected the precise conditions that indicated when a government emissions test was being run. Then, and only then, did the control software fully enable the anti-pollution devices fitted to the vehicle.

At all other times, the "road calibration" resulted in nitrogen oxide emissions up to 35 times higher than permitted by the US standard.

## Fudging the Benchmark

Attempts to mislead testers are unfortunately all too common in the IT industry.

Benchmarks are standardised ways of measuring the performance of IT systems but they are regularly gamed by manufacturers seeking a marketing edge.

In 2013 the technology enthusiast website AnandTech reported that many major smartphone manufacturers had written firmware that compared the name of the app currently running with a list of known benchmarks.

Normally, a smartphone's Central Processing Unit (CPU) is heavily self-monitored. It only runs at full speed for short bursts to avoid damage from overheating and to increase battery life.

But if a benchmark was detected, the CPU ran at full speed continuously. This slightly improved benchmark scores, but in a way that would result in flat batteries and burned pockets were it to be replicated for everything a smartphone does.

## Rogue Engineers?

Volkswagen's public statements to date have not attributed blame to specific individuals.

Bernd Osterloh, chairman of Volkswagen's work council and a member of the executive committee, said:

A small group has done damage to our company. We need a climate where mistakes are not hidden.

The idea that a small group of relatively junior engineers would have done this on their own is not consistent with how engineers build complex, safety-critical systems.

The basic engine management software was written by component supplier Bosch. The responsibility for configuring the software for the EA189 engine would have involved a substantial, multi-disciplinary team of engineers at Volkswagen, working with engineers at the supplier Bosch.

Before the engines could have gone into production, those engineers and their managers would have reviewed and approved the design and calibration of the engine management systems.

They would have also agreed upon, and employed, a systematic testing schedule. This would have involved testing on an engine-only rig, road testing on private grounds as well as testing on public roads.

The anti-pollution engineers would have been responsible for ensuring that the engine management system was sending appropriate commands to their components, and that their hardware was responding appropriately.

This kind of exhaustive testing is one of the reasons why developing new vehicle models costs billions of dollars and takes several years.

One possibility is that a large group of Volkswagen engineers conspired to falsify the written records of of this testing.

An alternative scenario is that accurate written testing records were made, showing that the pollution controls were inoperative in normal driving. These accurate records were reported through normal channels, and the engines went into production anyway.

It is very hard to imagine how either event could have occurred without the influence of senior managers.

German newspaper reports indicate Bosch may have informed Volkswagen about the illegality of its plans in 2007, and that senior management were informed about the issue in 2011.

## Rare Is the Whistleblower

The responsibility for the decision to deceive the emissions testers will ultimately rest some way up Volkswagen's management chain. But as well as the senior decision-makers, there is very likely to have been a much larger group of engineers who knew of the illegal deception, understood the consequences and chose not to reveal it to authorities or the media. The lack of whistleblowers from this larger group is striking.

The ethical duties of software engineers in these circumstances are, theoretically, quite clear. The Software Engineering Code of Ethics, agreed jointly by the Association for Computing Machinery (ACM) Institute of Electrical and Electronics Engineers (IEEE), states that a software engineer should:

> Disclose to appropriate persons or authorities any actual or potential danger to the user, the public, or the environment, that they reasonably believe to be associated with software or related documents.

While the code also addresses responsibilities to employers, including confidentiality, it makes clear the primacy of the public interest in cases where these ethical duties conflict:

> [...] in all these judgments concern for the health, safety and welfare of the public is primary; that is, the "Public Interest" is central to this Code.

Acting on this professional obligation, when it involves revealing an employer's unethical practices to regulators or the media, usually imposes a tremendous personal cost. As a consequence, examples of engineers blowing the whistle are very rare.

Engineer Salvador Castro informed the US Food and Drug Administration (FDA) about a potentially life-threatening flaw in his employer's infant incubators, after his employer did not fix the issue. He was fired and was unable to regain regular employment, despite the flaw being confirmed and a recall notice issued by the FDA.

As this example illustrates, the incentives for working engineers reward keeping quiet, not speaking out.

## Holding Individuals Accountable

As time goes on, there will be much interest in whether the more senior decision-makers responsible for the deception at Volkswagen are punished appropriately, given the consequences of their actions.

But to concentrate only on decision-makers lets the much larger group who knew something and did nothing off the hook.

It's time to look at the incentives for all engineers to disclose flawed systems that put the public at severe risk to the appropriate authorities (or the media).

Firstly, we need to find better ways to protect those whistleblowers who do come forward. But we should go further. We should seriously consider whether those who could, but do not, disclose dangerously flawed systems should, in some circumstances, face some kind of sanction.

# Tech Giants Would Like to Change Our Cities

*Richard Waters*

*In the following viewpoint, Richard Waters reports on Google's foray into "smart city" development—the effort to bring wide-reaching technological innovation into cities, changing how they're built and how they run—through an enterprise called Sidewalk Labs. Headed by Dan Doctoroff, who was deputy mayor of New York City under Michael Bloomberg, Sidewalk Labs is taking a "bottom-up" approach, launching "experimental projects that have the potential to catch on virally with large numbers of city dwellers." Waters discusses how smart city initiatives have failed in the past, as well as the municipal functions best suited to smart city–style intervention. Waters is a writer for the* Financial Times.

As you read, consider the following questions:

1. Why are some experts wary of Google's efforts to stake a claim in municipal infrastructure?
2. How does Larry Page, CEO of Google's parent company, Alphabet, believe the technology can reduce housing prices?
3. What are the six functions of city life that might be served by technological intervention, according to the author?

"Google and the Tech Industry Search for 'Smart City,'" by Richard Waters, The Financial Times Ltd., June 19, 2015. Reprinted by permission.

There is nothing new about trying to use internet-era technologies to make the world's cities function better. But Google's emergence on the scene—with a declared goal of making life better for billions of people—has brought new attention to a field that most experts say has been slow to deliver on its promises.

The internet search company's announcement last week that it had set up a division to develop "urban technologies" came with characteristic audacity. Under Dan Doctoroff, a former deputy mayor of New York City and chief executive of media group Bloomberg, the division will work on ideas that affect sweeping issues such as "cost of living, efficient transportation and energy usage" for many of the world's city dwellers, according to Larry Page, chief executive.

The grandness of the ambition provoked a reaction that has become familiar with Google's increasingly frequent forays into sweeping new areas of economic and social life. As one expert in the field—and self-professed fan of the company's efforts—says: "You can't help feeling there's a lot of hubris."

The initiative, called Sidewalk Labs, is shaping up to be different from much of the work that has been done by technology companies to create so-called smart cities. Mr Doctoroff wants to assemble small teams of experts to brainstorm ideas and launch experimental projects that have the potential to catch on virally with large numbers of city dwellers, according to Carlo Ratti, an expert on cities at the Massachusetts Institute of Technology who has been contacted by Google.

This kind of "bottom-up" approach has the potential to bring rapid change at low cost, he says—in contrast to the more centralised, "top-down" tech projects that cities have used in the past to reduce costs or improve the delivery of their services.

Google is far from being from the first technology company to see the huge potential market around smart cities. "I think they're a little late—IBM and others have marketed this idea for some time," says Ryan Chin, head of an initiative at MIT's Media Lab.

Much of the work has been focused on getting more value out of a city's assets by optimising their use, or on bringing greater efficiency to capacity planning for future investments, says Michael Dixon, general manager of IBM's initiative in the area.

Yet it has taken time to get results. "It's definitely been slower than people wanted," says Ruthbea Yesner Clarke, an analyst at IDC, the research firm.

Part of the reason, she says, is that the first wave of smart city technology coincided with a downturn that left many cities short of cash to back new projects.

Sheer complexity has also played a part. Projects often rely on a range of technologies, from using "internet of things" products such as sensors to gather and analyse massive amounts of data, to open databases of civic information. In densely populated places, projects that lead to changes in behaviour, such as new transport arrangements, also have unexpected knock- on effects in other areas.

If change is in the air, it owes a lot to a deeper knowledge of how life works inside the world's biggest cities, according to experts. "We've crossed a threshold in that there is a lot of data out there and it continues to grow exponentially," says Steve Koonin, head of a cities project at New York University who is among the people Mr Doctoroff has assembled to work on advisory boards for Sidewalk.

It also reflects a belief that pervasive new technologies such as smartphones and the cloud have laid a foundation for disruptive change. Ride-hailing service Uber has become a widely touted model for bottom-up change: by making car services cheaper and more convenient it could reduce the incentives for car ownership, with significant impacts on the way cities operate.

With its history of collecting and crunching large amounts of data, Google should be particularly suited to this field, says Mr Koonin—though this is likely to stir the privacy concerns that often accompany its most ambitious new projects.

Google has other assets that it could bring to bear on its urban ambitions: driverless cars, the Nest "smart homes" division that makes thermostats and smoke alarms, the Waze app for tracking traffic congestion, even the local broadband networks it is building

# The Bizarre, Bony-Looking Future of Algorithmic Design

Pick a building on the horizon—any building will do—and consider for a moment how it came to be. Long before construction began, there was an architect and a blueprint. The blueprint bore a design that came from an idea the architect had about how the building should look. The process by which an architect's idea becomes a blueprint that becomes a building is an example of explicit design. It's more or less how we've always built not just buildings, but the majority of the physical objects that surround us.

With generative design, a designer begins with an objective or set of objectives—the desired energy consumption for a building, for example, or the amount of sunlight a room should receive—and then lets algorithms take the reins on drafting solutions. This might be a big ask for designers, because when we build something, whether it's a skyscraper or a trash can, "we have a preconceived notion of how it looks," says [Jordan] Brandt. But a machine—Autodesk's software, in this instance—is an unbiased agent. "[It's] simply looking to optimize the criteria we set forward," says Brandt.

[G]enerative design is about trying things out and seeing what works. Crucially, however, it does so over the course of a few hours, as opposed to a few million years. "We're essentially running accelerated artificial evolution," says Brandt.

With Autodesk's Within Medical software, biomedical engineers are designing and 3-D printing surgical implants that are more organically structured and perform better in the body.

If this version of the future—one where algorithms are designers—comes with a dystopian ring, it's worth considering all the ways these design tools free up time for creators. By just speeding up the process by which we create motorcycle parts or knee joint implants, designers can more carefully consider what design objectives are most important and which could potentially perform better.

"The Bizarre, Bony-Looking Future of Algorithmic Design," by Margaret Rhodes, WIRED, September 23, 2015.

in a number of US cities. These are all part of a broad technology platform that could be applied, says Ms Clarke.

But to have an effect in such a vast and complex field, the company will also have to find new forms of leverage. That might include "accessing government data that isn't open yet," or trying to own "a particular piece of infrastructure, particularly data infrastructure" that would give it influence, says Mr Koonin.

For Mr Page, Sidewalk Labs could also address issues close to home. With the technology industry booming, a lack of affordable housing has become one of San Francisco's biggest problems, says Mr Chin. Google's private bus system to ferry its employees from the city to its offices in Silicon Valley has become a symbol of rising inequality and "created a lot of anxiety," he adds.

These issues have been on Mr Page's mind. In an interview with the Financial Times last year, he said it should be possible to achieve radical reductions in house prices in Silicon Valley. New types of building material and structure are among the issues on which Sidewalk will be focused, according to a person familiar with its plans.

With Google investors becoming restless at the company's spending on long-term projects, Mr Page said it had made only a "relatively modest investment" in its urban technology division, without revealing specific details. To have the kind of broad impact he hopes for, the company will either have to spend a lot more—or persuade a broad array of other companies and civic organisations that its vision for better urban living is worth backing.

## Targeted Areas in the "Smart City"

### Healthcare

Personalised treatments designed for patients use big data to comb through millions of medical records and pharmaceutical data. Tech companies hope this will help identify outbreaks and allow doctors to analyse how treatments will work.

## Traffic

Gridlock avoided through real-time data reduces congestion and emissions. IBM says that US traffic causes about 4.2bn hours of wasted commuting time and $87bn in extra fuel. Ride-hailing services such as Uber and Lyft are reducing the lure of car ownership.

## Energy

Grid models will predict demand and deploy energy more efficiently. The number of smart meters deployed by energy and water utilities to track and optimise household energy use will grow from 228m to more than a 1bn by the end of 2020, according to ABI research.

## Law Enforcement

Data analytics will be used to anticipate when and where criminal problems might occur. Companies say they can analyse data to understand patterns of incidents so resources can be allocated most efficiently.

## Construction

New construction materials and designs are set to make buildings cheaper, more flexible and more energy efficient. The advances could help solve problems such as affordable housing or changes of use.

## Water

Technology projects will modernise water systems and as a result reduce waste, improve efficiency and prepare for the growth of megacities. Water usage is increasing at twice the rate of population growth.

# Periodical and Internet Sources Bibliography

*The following articles have been selected to supplement the diverse views presented in this chapter.*

Tyler Cowen, "Automation Alone Isn't Killing Jobs," *New York Times,* April 5, 2014. https://www.nytimes.com/2014/04/06/business /automation-alone-isnt-killing-jobs.html.

Tyler Cowen, "The Robots Are Here," *Politico Magazine,* November 2013. http://www.politico.com/magazine/story/2013/11/the -robots-are-here-098995.

Garry Kasparov, "The Chess Master and the Computer," *New York Review of Books,* February 11, 2010. http://www .nybooks.com/articles/2010/02/11/the-chess-master-and-the -computer/?pagination=false.

Rem Koolhaas, "My Thoughts on the Smart City," European Commission, September 24, 2014. http://ec.europa.eu/archives /commission_2010-2014/kroes/en/content/my-thoughts-smart -city-rem-koolhaas.html.

Paul Krugman, "Building a Green Economy," *New York Times Magazine,* April 7, 2010. http://www.nytimes.com/2010/04/11 /magazine/11Economy-t.html?ref=magazine&pagewanted=all.

Gideon Lewis-Kraus, "The Great A.I. Awakening," *New York Times Magazine,* December 14, 2016. https://www.nytimes .com/2016/12/14/magazine/the-great-ai-awakening.html?_r=0.

Martin Lukacs, "New, Privatized African City Heralds Climate Apartheid," *Guardian,* January 21, 2014. https://www .theguardian.com/environment/true-north/2014/jan/21/new -privatized-african-city-heralds-climate-apartheid.

Casey Newton, "Speak, Memory," The Verge. http://www.theverge.com /a/luka-artificial-intelligence-memorial-roman-mazurenko-bot.

Steven Poole, "The Truth About Smart Cities: 'In the End, They Will Destroy Democracy'," *Guardian,* December 17, 2014. https:// www.theguardian.com/cities/2014/dec/17/truth-smart-city -destroy-democracy-urban-thinkers-buzzphrase.

Bryant Walker Smith, "Slow Down That Runaway Ethical Trolley," The Center for Internet and Society, January 12, 2015. http:// cyberlaw.stanford.edu/blog/2015/01/slow-down-runaway -ethical-trolley.

# For Further Discussion

**Chapter 1**

1. Do you think it is possible to regulate the tech industry without also curbing innovation? How?
2. Do you think there is anything wrong with disruption for disruption's sake? Explain the pros and cons of disruption.

**Chapter 2**

1. In the same way that nations around the world have collaborated to ratify compatible copyright laws, should world leaders now come together on an international bill of rights that applies to internet privacy?
2. How do you safeguard privacy as independent tech companies steward more and more personal data? Is it necessary to differentiate between sensitive and innocuous data points? Is that possible?

**Chapter 3**

1. Tech companies have created a new paradigm in which the line between corporate interest and social responsibility is blurred. How might government officials separate one from the other and determine which policy recommendations benefit the company's bottom line and which benefit society at large?
2. The internet has given rise to ultra-focused media platforms and created a forum where it can be hard to differentiate between legitimate and illegitimate sources. Do tech companies have an obligation to promote accuracy?

**Chapter 4**

1. Do you think the vision of a Google-owned, -designed, and (effectively) -governed city is utopian or dystopian? Explain your thinking.

2. Is it at all problematic that an industry that struggles to promote diversity wants to take the lead on cultural innovation, automation, and urbanization? Why or why not?

# Organizations to Contact

*The editors have compiled the following list of organizations concerned with the issues debated in this book. The descriptions are derived from materials provided by the organizations. All have publications or information available for interested readers. The list was compiled on the date of publication of the present volume; the information provided here may change. Be aware that many organizations take several weeks or longer to respond to inquiries, so allow as much time as possible.*

**The Center for Internet and Society at Stanford Law School**
559 Nathan Abbott Way
Stanford, CA 94305
website: http://cyberlaw.stanford.edu/contact

The Center for Internet and Society (CIS) brings together scholars, engineers, politicians, and entrepreneurs to explore the relationship between law and technology. CIS is focused on the following areas: architecture and public policy, copyright, free speech, privacy, and robotics.

**The Future of Life Institute**
website: https://futureoflife.org/contact

The Future of Life Institute studies the existential risks humans face: artificial intelligence, nuclear proliferation, biotechnology, and climate change. Through research and other actions, the institute works to develop "optimistic visions of the future."

## MIT Media Lab
77 Mass. Avenue, E14/E15
Cambridge, MA 02139
phone: (617) 253-5960
email: web-general@media.mit.edu
website: https://www.media.mit.edu

At the MIT Media Lab, designers, computer scientists, and scholars investigate—and reinvent—the relationship between human experience and technological innovation. The lab is focused on issues of ethical engineering, bionics, and affective computing.

## Murdough Center for Engineering Professionalism
Texas Tech University
Whitacre College of Engineering
Box 41023
Lubbock, TX 79409
phone: (806) 742-3525
email: webmaster.coe@ttu.edu
website: http://www.depts.ttu.edu/murdoughcenter

The Murdough Center for Engineering Professionalism—home of the National Institute for Engineering Ethics—is committed to exploring the ethical issues that attend engineering, promoting dialogues about best practices, and encouraging cooperation.

## One Hundred Year Study on Artificial Intelligence (AI100)
email: ai100-info@lists.stanford.edu
website: https://ai100.stanford.edu

Sponsored by Stanford, the One Hundred Year Study on Artificial Intelligence is an opportunity for a diverse group of leaders to anticipate the impact of AI on human livelihood over the next century.

## Pew Research Center
1615 L Street NW, Suite 800
Washington, DC 20036
phone: (202) 419-4300
website: http://www.pewresearch.org/contact-form/#General-Inquiry

One of the premiere nonpartisan research institutes (or "fact tanks") in the United States, the Pew Research Center regularly reports on the social, cultural, and political implications of the internet and technology.

## The Roosevelt Institute
570 Lexington Avenue, 5th Floor
New York, NY 10022
phone: (212) 444-9130
email: info@rooseveltinstitute.org
website: http://rooseveltinstitute.org

This progressive think tank is committed to investigating the interaction between technology and the workforce, posing questions and proposing solutions.

## Singularity University
NASA Research Park
Building 20 S. Akron Road
MS 20-1
Moffett Field, CA 94035
phone: (650) 200-3434
email: info@su.org

Singularity University is a Silicon Valley think tank. Its team looks at the ways nano- and biotechnology will affect human intelligence. Singularity has partnered with the World Health Organization to design and pursue social entrepreneurship endeavors.

**The Society on Social Implications of Technology**
website: http://ieeessit.org/about/input-form

The Society on Social Implications of Technology convenes professionals, scholars, and enthusiasts. Through publications, panels, and conferences, the society investigates the impact technological developments will have on human well-being.

**The Tow Center for Digital Journalism at Columbia's Graduate School of Journalism**
Columbia University Graduate School of Journalism
Pulitzer Hall, 6th Floor
116 and Broadway
New York, NY 10027
email: towcenter@columbia.edu
website: http://towcenter.org

Experts at the Tow Center for Digital Journalism puzzle over a complex question: How will technology alter the production and consumption of news? The center sponsors various research and educational initiatives.

**Urban-Think Tank**
c/o A. Brillembourg
155 E. 72 Street, Apt. 13C
New York, NY, 10021
phone: (646) 206-1042
website: http://u-tt.com

Urban-Think Tank is committed to pushing the boundaries of social architecture and development through various outlets, including teaching, filmmaking, and publishing.

# Bibliography of Books

Tyler Cowen, *Average Is Over: Powering America Beyond the Age of the Great Stagnation.* New York, NY: Dutton, 2013.

Joi Ito and Jeff Howe, *Whiplash: How to Survive Our Faster Future.* New York, NY: Grand Central Publishing, 2016.

Kevin Kelly, *What Technology Wants.* New York, NY: Viking, 2010.

Ray Kurzweil, *The Age of Spiritual Machines: When Computers Exceed Human Intelligence.* New York, NY: Penguin, 1999.

Katherine Losse, *The Boy Kings: A Journey into the Heart of the Social Network.* New York, NY: Free Press, 2012.

Dan Lyons, *Disrupted: My Misadventure in the Start-Up Bubble.* New York, NY: Hachette, 2016.

Antonio García Martínez, *Chaos Monkeys: Obscene Fortune and Random Failure in Silicon Valley.* New York, NY: HarperCollins, 2016.

Evgeny Morozov, *To Save Everything, Click Here: The Folly of Technological Solutionism.* New York, NY: Public Affairs, 2013.

Alec Ross, *The Industries of the Future.* New York, NY: Simon & Schuster, 2016.

Klaus Schwab, *The Fourth Industrial Revolution.* New York, NY: Crown Business, 2017.

Brad Stone, *The Everything Store: Jeff Bezos and the Age of Amazon.* New York, NY: Little, Brown and Company, 2013.

# Index

## F

Facebook, 22, 23, 24, 25, 26,
   27, 28, 29, 46–51, 56, 96,
   100, 101, 102, 103, 104,
   109, 134, 148
   lobbying efforts by, 85–93
   and online terrorist
      recruitment, 60–62
   and privacy policy, 55–56
fake news, 99, 101–102, 103,
   104, 105, 109
filter bubbles, 99–105, 113
Floridi, Luciano, 72–76
Fusion, 23
FWD lobbying coalition, 85–93

## G

Gates, Bill, 18, 136, 139, 144
gender gap in tech industry, 83
generative design, 162
Go, 20
Goldberg, Jason, 31, 32, 33
Gonzales, Mario Costeja,
   68–71
Google, 23, 24, 25, 28, 46, 47,
   48, 49, 51, 56, 80, 82, 100,
   101, 104, 137, 150–151,
   161, 163
   DeepMind, 20
   and lobbying, 88
   and privacy policy, 55–58
   and "right to be forgotten,"
      68–71, 72–76
   and "smart cities," 159–164

Greenberg, Julia, 60
Griswold, Alison, 43

## H

hackathons, 82
hate speech, 60, 111, 113,
   119–120
Hawking, Stephen, 18, 138,
   139, 144, 148
Hobbes, Thomas, 124, 126–127

## I

IBM, 137, 148, 160, 161, 164
*Innovator's Dilemma, The*, 30
ISIS, 60–62

## J

Johnson, Shontavia, 94–98
Joy, Bill, 18

## K

Katz, Rita, 60
Koonin, Steve, 161, 163
Kurzweil, Ray, 18

## L

Lapowsky, Issie, 88
Levy, Paul, 54–58
lobbying by tech giants, 85–93
Locke, John, 124, 127
Losse, Kate, 85–93
Love, Bradley, 17–21
Lyft, 39, 41, 164

# M

MacKinnon, Rebecca, 48
Maney, Kevin, 13
Marcus, Bonnie, 83
Markey, Jenn, 34
Martindale, Jon, 99–105
McCarthy, John, 142
Merkel, Robert, 154–158
Microsoft, 25, 48, 58, 148
Minsky, Marvin, 142
Moore, Martin, 45–51
Morfit, Simon, 79–84
Mulpuru, Sucharita, 33, 36
Musk, Elon, 18, 136, 139, 148

# N

network neutrality, 114

# O

Olson, Parmy, 56
Orenstein, James, 65–66
Osborne,George, 49
Osterloh, Bernd, 156

# P

Page, Larry, 160, 163
Palihapitiya, Chamath, 87
Pariser, Eli, 99, 105
Pishevar, Shervin, 39
privacy, 14, 41, 50, 51, 54–58, 65, 67–71, 115, 116, 118, 161

# R

Reda, Susan, 30–37
Reisinger, Don, 37
Rhodes, Margaret, 162
"right to be forgotten," 67–71, 72–76
Rochester, Nathaniel, 142
Rossman, John, 32, 33
Russell, Stuart, 143
Rutherford, Ernest, 142
Ryssdal, Kai, 19

# S

Samsung smart TV, 55
San Francisco Citizens Initiative for Technology and Innovation, 82
Seiff, Ken, 33, 34, 35
self-driving cars, 13–14, 137, 139, 144, 148, 161
Shaheen, Susan, 43
Shannon, Claude, 142
sharing economy/sharing economy firms, 38–44
Sidewalk Labs, 159, 160, 161, 163
Silverman, Scott, 32
"smart cities," 159–164
Snapchat, 22, 23, 24, 25
Snowden, Edward, 57
social media
and combating online terrorist recruitment, 59–62